NELL DUNN was born in London on 9 June 1936, the youngest of two sisters. She was educated at a convent until the age of 14, when she left without taking any exams. Dunn once said to her father: 'You should have given me a proper education! I can't even spell!' He replied: 'But darling you are so wonderful and your spelling is so original!' In 1957, she married Jeremy Sandford, who wrote *Cathy Come Home*, and two years later they moved to Battersea. There she worked in a sweet factory, had three sons and began writing short stories, which appeared in the *New Statesman*.

When the stories were collected as *Up the Junction* in 1963, they won the John Llewellyn Rhys Prize and were subsequently made into two films, one by Ken Loach. *Talking to Women* was Dunn's second book, written 'because I felt so lost, I wanted to know how other people were doing, and most of them were equally lost, really.' In 1967 she published *Poor Cow*. 'I don't want to be down and out all the time,' Joy, the main character, says, 'I want — I don't know what I do fucking want but I dream about driving a car, that I'm in this big car driving around.' The novel was a bestseller and was made into a film by Ken Loach with Carol White and Terence Stamp.

In 1971 Dunn separated from Sandford, and in the 1970s wrote two more novels and began writing plays. In 1977, she met the American computer mathematician Dan Oestreicher – they would be together for 35 years and would spend every night together but maintain separate houses. Her second play, *Steaming*, set in a Turkish bath in London with an all-female cast, opened at the Theatre Royal Stratford in 1981 before it transferred to the West End and Broadway. In 1985 Joseph Losey made it into a film – it would be his last – with Vanessa Redgrave. On the birth of her grandson Cato in 1991, Dunn made another book of conversations, this time on the subject of grandmothers, and in 1996, she returned to the character of Joy in the novel *My Silver Shoes*. In 2009, Oestreicher died of lung cancer and Dunn became a patron of Dignity in Dying, which campaigns for more choice and control over end of life decisions. She continued to write plays until *Home Death* in 2011. She lives in London, with her dachshunds Iris and Tulip.

ALI SMITH was born in Inverness and lives in Cambridge. Her fiction has been translated into forty languages.

.

Talking to Women

Nell Dunn

Silver Press

FOR FRANCES

CONTENTS

INTRODUCTION

TALKING TO WOMEN was the book Nell Dunn published between the hugely seminal works *Up the Junction* (1963) and *Poor Cow* (1967). Like them, it was unprecedented for its era, and era-forming. That it's back in print for the first time since it came out in 1965 is cause for celebration: it also gives us a chance half a century later to take new stock of its complex inheritance and the courage and honesty that's this book's lifeblood. When it comes to voice and the making of space for it, this book is both part and source of hard-won social metamorphosis.

In it Dunn idiomatically transcribes nine informal interviews she recorded with young women she happened to be near and around in the year 1964, friends across the class system, from factory worker Kathy Collier to socialite heiress Suna Portman, with a particular eye to women marking themselves out creatively, against the odds; 'these girls', according to Dunn's preface, share more than just a common time and age; they've each 'severed themselves from some of the conventional forms of living and thinking'. A couple of them are names we recognise fifty years on; some have been lost then found again as artists and writers. Dunn titles each interview equally with each woman's first name alone ('Pauline', 'Kathy', 'Frances'). The women rub shoulders with each other in a spatially sociable and social work.

'Do you find communication a problem?' the young Nell Dunn, in her late twenties, says in 1964 to the more knowing and elder (well, just past thirty) Paddy Kitchen. 'Yes,' Paddy says. 'I'm not very good at talking.' It's almost comic: right then Dunn herself was already on her way to becoming one of the pioneers of postwar literary voice, already one of the clearest voices in the articulation and the formation of the pressing changes in shifting social understanding about class and gender. Paddy had published her first novel and was on her way to what would be a lifetime's worth of fiction, biography, art criticism, arts administration revolution and art and literacy teaching. Communication, you might say, was what they were all about. But this was a time when what women might or might not say or do was shifting too, and reading it now it's a revelation again quite how pioneering a work *Talking to Women* was and what substantial and endemic problematics its act of conscious articulation faced.

Sheila Rowbotham, in *Promise of a Dream* (2000), recalls how 'little cultural space existed at this time for expressing the sexual freedoms emerging among young women of my generation. We were beginning to want relationships with men on quite new terms, yet were barely conscious of these needs. I was fascinated by the discussions of sex which appeared in Nell Dunn's *Talking to Women*. For the first time I was seeing in print perceptions I recognised from intimate conversations with women friends.' What Rowbotham says next, in a remark about her lover the economist Bob Rowthorne's take on the book, is the giveaway: 'But Bob dismissed it as frivolous and not political.'

Not political. Well, this book opens with Dunn's interview with Pauline Boty, herself a challenger of preconception in politics, class and gender, who was pretty much the only UK female Pop artist to make an impact and was certainly the only contemporary UK artist addressing Pop Art's imagery with any nod to gender questioning and analysis. She was working with a political heft that can't be denied. But after her death from cancer at the age of 28 (just a year after the publication of the interview in this book) Boty's vital and astonishing artwork all but disappeared, was soon forgotten, much of it lost.

Many images of Boty herself, as a 'person', a 'sitter', were collected by the National Portrait Gallery. At the end of last year the gallery held 29 images of Boty, which happened to be invaluable to anyone looking for information about or reproduction of her works since Boty was canny enough to place her (very beautiful) self in front of her art – as part of her art – when photographers came to the studio to take their (very saleable) images of her. But also at the end of last year the National Portrait Gallery acquired its very first Boty artwork, a 1958 self-portrait in stained glass. The portrait is in the form of a lightbox. It transforms figuration more usually associated with both religious iconography and the glass panelling more usually found above the doors of every 1930s semi-detached suburban house, into a fusion of medieval, renaissance, Pre-Raphaelite, even Picasso-like associations. A green plant-form, like a dark and mighty lifeforce, is revealed at the core of the body of the woman in the portrait; an efflorescence rises through her from it. At the same time, the face of the woman is split, cut right across – blocked at the mouth – by a slant of metal.

Her lower lip pushes back against it and under it, full and human.

*

Nell Dunn began writing fiction in the late 1950s, composing a number of short vignettes around the everyday life and the people she met when she moved to Battersea and began working in a sweet factory. After leaving convent school at 14, and with an education picked up here and there across the world, Dunn had crossed the river away from her own upper-class background, from Chelsea to Battersea, and settled there. 'It was no big experimental business, you know,' she told Selina Robertson who interviewed her in 2016 about crossing the classes at a time when such border-crossing was nigh-unheard-of. 'I liked it and I moved in.' Some of these short pieces were first published in the *New Statesman* then went on to form the body of *Up the Junction*, a book whose radically open structure allows it to be a collection of short fiction *and* a different kind of novel both at once, as well as a work that nods, but very lightly, to autobiography and documentary observation.

Its subject matter, its sexual frankness and its marked unsentimentality, its refusal to provide any fake narrative payoff and its revelation of working class power – especially its portrayal of the forthrightness of working class women, their strength, their unpretentious spirit – ignited a public reaction part scandalised, part ecstatic. It became a runaway bestseller.

'A refugee from smarter and more moneyed circles' is how her friend Margaret Drabble puts it in her introduction to Dunn's equally visceral and open-structured novel *Poor Cow*. Drabble describes elsewhere Dunn's gift for openness when it comes to the given shapes of things both literary and worldly: 'She was lucky in many ways, not having a formal literary education. It gives her an extraordinary freshness of eye and ear and means she's much less burdened with all sorts of baggage . . . There's something very unconstructed about her way of looking at the world . . . It's very hopeful.'

'I hope to learn to be more open,' is how Dunn concludes her 1977 book *Living Like I Do*, 'a book about alternative families' and another interview book or voice-work, one which makes of structure a communal dialogue, or multilogue.

Dunn was drawn, from the start, to communality, shared talk (and later she'd be drawn specifically to script work, writing *Steaming* (1981) and *Cancer Tales* (2002) for theatre production). Her art — one where an expert instinct for edit and for the energy that radiates off perfectly judged juxtaposition comes together with a talent for hearing and relaying with an uncanny authenticity the rhythms and resonances of idiom — is ignited by voice, especially by voice more usually given no societal, literary or aesthetic power or space but whose authority, as soon as you hear it, is unquestionable.

'There, up the junction', Drabble writes, Dunn wrote about a world 'where women did not depend on male patronage, where they went their own ways, sexually and financially, where there was plenty of work, so much work that they could afford to be cheeky, rebellious, loud-mouthed . . . It seemed a real world, where women could lead real lives. They did not seem oppressed, despite their low pay. There was a sense of matriarchy.' Over her lifetime of writing, Dunn has come back again and again to the power specifically in the voices of women. 'The women really ruled the roost in those days,' she writes in a piece about what she found when she did that forbidden thing and crossed from one side of London to the other. 'Sometimes a man had to change his name to the woman's to fit in with the family.' In the early 1960s the breakthrough radicalism of *Up the Junction* lay in to whom it gave voice as well as what it voiced, at a time when such things *just weren't said.*

'I like talking,' its heiress-turned-factory-worker character tells a casual male lover in a chapter that's almost all in the voice of that lover. It's a rare moment in this book of the narrator's individual voice surfacing; Dunn's narrator's voice is more usually a fusion-delivery of the voices (female and male) round her and also of the sounds and sights of the time: a fragment of pop song, a bird singing above an empty house on an old bomb site, the shreds of words and colours on an advertising hoarding; so that reading becomes a kind of sensory collage, a listening vision, one which reveals the ironies, truths, comedies, foulnesses, the losses, the cruelties, the sometimes funny sometimes fuck-you survival, the social and natural realities, in an unforced transcribing, life drawn from the life. 'We had this woman from the WVS come to tell us what to do if they dropped the H-bomb on us. "First thing," she says: "fill your bath with water." "We haven't got no bath, love," I says. That put her right in it.'

Everything becomes sensory in Dunn's writing via a narrator who can hold romanticism and bathos together in their simultaneity simply by telling it as it is 'as the sun set over the power station'. *Poor Cow* takes this further, developing the oral/aural energy of *Up the Junction* into a mêlée of first person and third person which goes to make up the individual: a shifting palette of things heard, overheard, thought, spoken, not-spoken, written, idiolectic, formal, casual, internal and external, all making for a constant dialogue at work in the individual while blurring words like individual, communal and societal into one state, so that individual comes to mean a united and simultaneously fragmented matter, voice as history, as life – voice being what we are.

VI

'I want to be somebody people listen to,' the character Queenie – who's an old 'business girl' or a nobody, or a societal discard, or a lifeforce, a different history, a different kind of head of state, and a real and vital person without whom there's no living, without whom life disappears – says at her most fractious and near-ruined in Dunn's 1974 novel *Tear His Head off His Shoulders*. Dunn isn't just open to voice, she knows its worth. She knows the forces that work to silence it, or can decide not to hear it.

It's voice that matters, it's voice that *is* matter in her work, the live and speaking interact of voice and voices. In her decades of telling it as it is, Dunn's life project has been dialogue in action, in a part-meditative, part-communal opposition to silence and all the silencers.

*

Talking, naturally (as well as talking naturally), is one of the central preoccupations of *Talking to Women*. Its common theme is the radical necessity of giving and having voice. Its interviewees admit and repeat both desire and difficulty in just, well, talking. While they do, something fundamental shifts in the act of the book: the possibilities of talk, and what talk means, shift as we read it.

Dunn interviews instinctually rather than fixedly, working with a set of questions which may or may not turn up from interview to interview. By and large each interview is allowed to take its natural direction. She asks about morality, politics, economic survival. She asks about life lived with or without the having of children, whether this is a choice or a desire, and the economics of it (the interviewees respond right across the range from negative to positive when it comes to what they think to maternity). She asks about marriage: is it out of date? She asks repeatedly

about the meaning of passion and whether her interviewees think passion is about sex, whether they 'think sex is
tremendously important'. She asks if they're frightened of
dying. She asks about hope. She asks about love. She asks
about class, creativity, domesticity, and the everyday politics of role. She asks nine young women in their twenties
or just touching thirty what they imagine the future will
bring them. The answers they give are 'as varied as being
alive'. The separate interviews fuse into a vision of one
great shared and galvanisingly varied voice, intimate but
still somehow profoundly social, and a reader is privileged
not just to be there but to be so openly invited into this
astonishing, funny, still stunningly frank fifty years later,
sometimes painful, always thoughtful, multiple tête-à-
tête.

What comes to light, even as Ann (the experimental
novelist Ann Quin) is saying the words 'verbally we can't
really communicate', and Edna (O'Brien) is commenting
on how 'most people are ashamed of saying what's close
to them', and Emma (Charlton) is lamenting how 'human
beings are totally unequipped' and endlessly stymied by
'this inability to communicate about things you really care
about', is the unashamed intimacy, the articulacy of each
speaker, up against the pressure on each one, the pressure
even just on language.

Sex is 'only another language really,' Antonia (Simon)
says. 'Passion to me involves communication on all levels,'
Ann says. 'By actually marrying someone you're saying
something that you can't say in any other way,' says Pauline who has recently married her husband only days after
they met because 'he accepted me intellectually . . . the
first man I could really talk very freely to . . . someone who
liked women and to whom they weren't kind of things.'
Every one of the women interviewed knows that role, and

especially gender role, pressurises what it's acceptable or possible to say. Every one, at one point or another in her interview, finds herself torn between the attractions and the given script of role, and the repulsions, the wreckage that comes of accepting the given societal script. Emma is articulate about how playing the role currently expected of her reduces both men *and* women. 'Even if I think they are unattractive I often say things which I know it would suit them to hear. But really that's a form of looking down on them.' Frances (Chadwick) knows what she thinks about 'dreadful things in women's magazines making it appear that the whole point of a woman's life is the time when she's attractive to a man'; she connects this to 'being brought up to feel a second-class citizen, inferior to a man in every way, encouraged to think of oneself as the object of a man's pursuit and therefore with no vital life of your own.' Edna, whose 'first and initial body thoughts were blackened by the fear of sin', in a kind of echo-response to Frances, comments that 'a man must feel very sad when he can't impregnate every desirable woman in the world.'

It's a witty read: 'How can a man be unfaithful in your hand-knitted jumper?' 'I've often thought what I really need is a wife.' It's an anarchic read: 'The older you get the less need there is for society's morality, because you have established your own fierce rigorous morality.' It reveals the guilts, the social and economic inequalities, the fragilities and insecurities, and the courage simply in the act of speaking at all, of every one of the women interviewed. Is it possible, too, that Ann is taking Dunn gently to task when it comes to literary notions of class ('I hate this sort of thing of setting up working class people and so on I really do. People are people to me . . . I get sick to death of it being – well ever since the novel in England has been concerned with class . . . I think it's been overdone')?

Dunn asks Ann whether she regrets having had an abortion (still illegal till 1967 – the impact of Dunn's writing is one of the reasons the abortion laws shifted and changed). It takes an experimental novelist like Ann Quin to formulate choice out of no choice: 'It was something that I'd chosen to do, and there seemed no alternative therefore I went ahead and did it,' where it takes a writer like Dunn to hold at a steady balance, at the core of this quicksilver interview, the line Ann walks between assurance and vulnerability, going her own way on her own terms against the odds, clearly costly even though she speaks so lightly. This book's brilliance lies on the one hand in the coruscating frankness of each speaker, and on the other in its gift of what's beneath what's being said.

'You know, a man in bed at night, and cornflakes and all that. I think I despise it as well as wanting it.' The interview with Edna is a rich and brilliant tour-de-force, close to monologue, revealing a young thinker anciently wise to both her own and society's fantasies. Dunn allows her the space. More: she can sense that Edna's aesthetic is sourced in a truly visceral state that's been disciplined into something calmer, a curiosity that's all acceptance: 'Somehow I know,' Dunn says to Edna, 'that you'd be just as interested if I fell down drunk and got slapped in the face as if I was alright.'

With Kathy (Collier) Dunn's dialogue sharpens. 'I thought about gassing myself,' Kathy says. 'It'd cost you two or three bob in the meter,' Dunn says. It's funny and it isn't. Several of the nine women interviewed here have contemplated suicide. Two of them will die by their own hands; Frances was already gone before the book even saw publication and Ann at 37 less than a decade later. Married at 16 herself, Kathy notes how 'it's every young girl's wish to get married, isn't it?' Dunn asks her what her biggest mistake has been. 'Getting married when I was 16.'

Kathy has a passion for tolerance, and an intolerance for lies; this tricky combination makes her own unspoken preoccupations rise to the surface of what she's saying. The interview with Pauline ranges across many subjects: creative inspiration, childhood, pressures, drugs, depressions, self-worth, self-definition, back round to inspiration again, but its real subject is utterance, and Pauline's relationship with utterance. What she says out loud is telling enough in itself. A section which begins 'I felt guilty about having an ugly cunt' goes on to become a description of when she 'was very little surrounded by my brothers and everything, who kept yelling "Shut up, you're only a girl,"' then ends in thoughts about being expected to be/made to be/choosing to be a 'dumb blonde'.

The multiple meaning of a word like dumb isn't lost in a book about talking. The interview, the antithesis of dumbness, so clever, earnest, joyful, fragile, darting, layered and engaged, is scattered with violence and the repeated casual use of the words 'kill' and 'scream'. Edna too, in an interview laced with violent and visceral imagery uses the word when Dunn asks her about 'being a writer and having children' and Edna talks about a nourishment that involves scraping marrow out of bones, about half the time 'being a mother', and the other half wanting 'not to know that they're alive', because 'being a writer is being a writer constantly'. This state of split self, she suggests, 'that's why women's books and writing, modern women, read as screams.'

So *Talking to Women* is also a joltingly frank 20th-century creative handbook, one of the first books to address the complications of the female self fragmented by and determined to change, or at least ask questions about, the prescribed notions of what women's creativity should or shouldn't be. 'That's what's so marvellous, that's why the feeling is so terribly good, the feeling of creating,' Dunn says to Suna (Portman). 'Because you're using every inch of yourself . . . to me it's the only time I'm really alive, creating.' If Frances thinks scrubbing a floor 'isn't so different from sitting down and writing a poem', Suna has 'a real need, a tactile need to take hold of things by solidifying them, either in paint or in words'. Creativity is a life and death matter to her. 'I just feel paper, skin and paper, between me and death the whole time.'

The book, revelatory about its interviewees, is also revelatory about 'Nell'. It's in the interview with Paddy that Dunn herself most slips forward; something pivots between them and it's rather like Paddy is leading Nell out. 'I'm not very good at talking,' Paddy says, and proceeds to listen, like every good talker.

This is the interview in which Dunn says the following. 'I find that one's constantly feeling what is one doing shutting oneself up in rooms writing books when there are plenty of books. Shouldn't one be out fighting for freedom?' But it's freedom that's at stake, in this book of interviews. Emma tells Dunn, 'I do wish that I hadn't been such a pioneer. I wish I'd been a little later . . . My mother was a social outcast because of me.' 'What do you get most out of doing now?' Dunn asks her. 'Talking, I suppose,' she says. Talking is, for Dunn, and for everyone in dialogue with anyone, a politics of the personal, the social, the communal. In this way, it's a place to live. 'This is what I mean by passion, sort of heart-to-heart really,' Dunn says to Ann. 'This is the highest thing we can have in a life is this passionate relationship with another human being.' This book is a work of that pioneering passion.

Pauline, a pioneer herself, muses in her interview on how she probably won't enjoy being forty but how fifty will be a lot better. At the same time, she looks the present in the eye, 'living my life as though I'd probably only got a few more years to live – because the bomb was going to drop and I found this terribly exciting – not the bomb but living for today.' She did indeed have only a year.

In this book, here's her voice.

Here's a few hours of pure open-eared life with each of the women in this book, through which time, thought, culture, place, articulation, its difficulties and its ease all surface. In a hashtag soundbite time it's a reminder of the complexity of any exchange, never mind any individual; at a time of deep division nationally and internationally it's a reminder of the richness and vitality of dialogue at every level of communication.

Here are all their voices, more than fifty years on, as alive as any shout in the street right now, telling us, if we're listening, what needed to change, what did change and what didn't, what they gained, what we gained, what they gave us, what not to lose, and what it means and it's meant all along in all the ways to be talking to women.

ALI SMITH
April 2018

PREFACE

If these girls have anything in common it is a belief in personal fulfilment – that a woman's life should not solely be the struggle to make men happy but more than that a progress towards the development of one's own body and soul.

As Daniel Deronda tells Gwendolen Harleth that she should sing for the 'private joy' instead of the public ear so these girls have severed themselves from some of the conventional forms of living and thinking, in trying to find what for them are the 'private joys' of life.

N.D.
1964

PAULINE

Twenty-five

NELL Something I feel very much is suddenly wishing that one had never got started on this business of being an artist and that one could return to being a completely free person that no one wants to know about or see, or is interested in. Do you get this feeling ever?

PAULINE Well, no, because I never expect people to know who I am. Except there has been a slight change recently when I've been in the company of people who are well known and they never know who I am, I mean, if someone knows about you, someone's heard of you and you're slightly famous, you know, then you're worth talking to and if you're not, then you're not, sort of thing and I sit there completely quiet and think, 'Well I've done something too.' That's the only time – it's only begun to happen to me.

NELL Do you find that it's well-known people who care if you've done something or not?

PAULINE No, but there are some people who I know who really do – they find people – well it's a sort of snob thing really, you know. They think that if you've made a name for yourself in one way or another then you must be more interesting than somebody who hasn't. And maybe

1

it's true. I'm never very good socially in any way unless I get sort of completely lost in something and then begin talking but otherwise I'm very tense. And no one will bother with you. Because from their point of view I suppose, you're not bothering with them. And also you haven't got something which is working for you which is a particular name, you know, and they haven't got a common ground to talk to you, because you're sort of nobody.

NELL But the man who rang up and commissioned the Christine Keeler painting, didn't that suddenly make you feel neurotic that you'd got to carry out a commission rather than just spend the day doing what you wanted to do?

PAULINE I much prefer things like that really, because I'm basically terribly lazy and I like being forced to do something – in the first place I love a challenge and I think 'marvellous', you know and then you begin to go through the torture bit afterwards but at first my reaction is 'great'.

NELL That's quite true and then one wishes one had never taken it on. But you never have a kind of yearning, when you're in the middle of a film or something that you could – that you were just an ordinary housewife with ten children?

PAULINE Never.

NELL You just don't see yourself at all in that role?

PAULINE I'd be so bored, I really would. I couldn't stand it.

NELL You don't think you'll ever become that?

PAULINE I hope not. But if I did it would be because I wanted to. At the moment I can't conceive of wanting to. But if I did do it, if it happened to me, I would have wanted it to happen.

NELL Do you think of the future or the present or the past most?

PAULINE I think of the present. Not much about the future. Well only in terms of sort of like I found myself sort of living my life as though I'd probably only got a few more years to live — because the bomb was going to drop and I found this terribly exciting — not the bomb but living for today. I rather enjoyed this really in a way, you know. But then I suddenly thought 'well perhaps it won't, you know,' it's just that . . . I think the threat of it makes you much more aware of now and what you're doing now and are you enjoying yourself in a way, you see. I think enjoying yourself is terribly important, though lots of people enjoy just working and things like that. Some people enjoy being miserable.

NELL What do you enjoy mostly?

PAULINE Well most of all — I enjoy nothing most of all . . . well, it takes two forms, it's either when you're so involved in doing something or being something that all your reactions are completely straight, I mean you don't think mentally or you don't react completely physically, it's just that all of you goes towards something. I suppose it's a sort of Zen thing. Or else just when you're sitting, or walking, doing anything that you're totally involved in.

NELL Yes, but I also think one has to be involved in someone.

PAULINE Well, I've been thinking about this lately, I just don't know, I find I have a fantasy image which is sort of like — one of my things is I really like making other people happy which might be an egotistical thing because they think, 'What a lovely girl!' but it's also there's a kind of image that I feel that I don't want people to sort of touch me — I suppose I'm almost frightened of being killed by people in a funny kind of way. I don't mean physically particularly — well it's physically as well — so I always like to feel that I am floating by and just occasionally seeing them and everything and it all sort of was lovely.

NELL Do you find that people drain you in any way? I find that when I go out and see a lot of people I'm tired myself for about five days.

PAULINE I think they do it – well, one of the most terribly difficult things I find is being social – when I first meet people who are strangers I can't relax at all. I have to know people for about four or five months before I can really relax but this might be an inferiority thing. When I was teaching for instance, after about – I mean the first term I used to be sick every time I came home I was so nervous – but after about the first six months or something I just went and had a ball all the time, you know.

NELL Do you think that acting has given you a lot of physical confidence?

PAULINE I think it might have probably helped a lot. And also I think it's nice seeing yourself being somebody else which isn't quite you but which is all based on you, because it's always based on you, in acting I think. But you've assumed another identity in a way so that you can show yourself much much more because you're not being yourself, you're saying, well really I'm supposed to be Anne Smith or something, and so you can really be much more yourself.

NELL You mean that it isn't really an escape from yourself, it's giving yourself another dimension?

PAULINE Well, I think it can be a release. I don't think it's giving yourself another dimension because you can only use the dimensions you have had, because I think it's based on the past you and the you now. It can never be a future you, I don't think. Yes, it could, perhaps it might be sometimes without you knowing it. I don't know, it's terribly difficult, that's a time thing. Somebody once told me after seeing me on the stage that they thought I moved terribly well, and I didn't know this and this made me feel terribly pleased. I think it's very nice to move well.

NELL And is the admiration nice?

PAULINE Well, I don't think you really get admiration. I think that you might get people who think it's marvellous to be an actress because they think of it as being glamorous but that's really got nothing to do with anything. I mean that's a completely fake thing. I think one of the terrible things about people setting out with actresses – I think this is mainly to do with girls more than men, is that they are kind of taken up with the glamour idea or 'I'm on the stage' you know, all this kind of thing, which I think I – I would like admiration. But I would hate to become terribly aware of it. If someone is being terribly effusive of me or something I've done then I shut off because you mustn't let yourself be affected by this.

NELL Why, do you think you'd get conceited, or what?

PAULINE Because it's very easy to get things out of proportion, and really and truly if you think about it, there are millions of other people who are much better than you anyway. And – well, I think it can be very destructive.

NELL And what about mental confidence – do you think that's a different thing from physical confidence?

PAULINE Oh, yes. Well, I think they're all interrelated. But probably one of the reasons I married Clive was because he really was – this might be something in me too because I'm very much inclined to play a role that someone sets for me particularly when I first meet people – to accept me quite as a human being you know, with a mind, and he accepted me intellectually which men find very difficult.

NELL Why? Men think of you just as a pretty girl you mean?

PAULINE No, they just find it embarrassing when you

start talking about – I've met so many men who get slightly embarrassed – they're a bit square probably. If you – well, for instance you know there are lots of women who are intellectually cleverer than lots of men but it's difficult for lots of men to ever accept this idea, and they often feel, 'Well anyway I'm a man and being a man is lots better than being a woman.'

NELL If you start talking about ideas and things they just think you're putting it on?

PAULINE Well, not that you're putting it on, they just find it slightly embarrassing and you aren't doing the right thing, you know. But they have to be a bit square really to think like that.

NELL What do they want you to talk about?

PAULINE I think most people want you to listen to them. Which I quite like at first, very much, because I love finding out about people. I'm interested about what people have done and how they live, all things like that.

NELL Do you feel that one should try to make the world a better place?

PAULINE Well, I still get terrible bouts – I used to call it sort of social conscience and – I mean if Goldwater becomes president I'll especially do it, but I want to do a picture about America which would be a – very much on that kind of side you know because of what's happening there and everything, but I again feel like I think so many people feel, you know, that it's a hopeless sort of thing, what can you do and if I really felt 'oh God there are starving millions in . . .' you know, I used to torture myself with this when I was a teenager and I should think 'well this is just really masochism because I'd go out there and do something if I really was going to' . . . and I still haven't. But well, yes, one should try to really – it all depends on what you think of as better. Hitler probably believed that he was going to make the world a better place.

NELL Do you think it's possible to stay with one man all your life?

PAULINE I think it's possible.

NELL Do you think women can endure life without love?

PAULINE Well, I think it's true of men as well, but many people have to.

NELL I don't really think it's true of men. I think they get sort of involved in their work and that they don't care but I think a woman's life becomes rather pointless.

PAULINE Well, I think that there's a lot of things that have been imposed on poor men and I think women are much better off in some ways because they haven't been told: 'You've got to go out and get a job and you've got to be masterful and you've got to be all this,' you know, from when they were very young they've had much more time to indulge themselves and find out about themselves and their emotional reactions to various things and things like that, you see and also they're tough, that's very nice for women but personally, you know, I really feel that love's terribly important to everybody and I don't mean romantic love or anything I mean, say, love of things or love of, say, flowers or love of machines or anything like that, you know, generalised sort of love, I think that's terribly important to people.

NELL Do you think for having this extra time women are often more interesting than men?

PAULINE No. I think they're more intriguing in little ways. They're terribly intriguing in the ways like they react to things and sort of materials and things like this – but I think they're terribly inclined to be – well they're allowed to be much lazier and they aren't taught to be competitive except physically with other women – they've got to

7

be prettier than all the other girls and women and all this kind of business but I find it easier to talk to men simply because they are probably engaged in a much more competitive world and because they're often much more involved with ideas and they've also been forced to develop themselves mentally more than women have. I often get embarrassed when talking to women because of this. Yet I've always sort of worshipped women in a funny sort of way. I've always thought they were terribly beautiful.

NELL Are you still bound by the conventions you were brought up in or have you a sort of code of your own?

PAULINE Well, there are certain conventions that of course I'm not bound by that my father tried to vaguely impose because he had a lot of Victorian ideas. He didn't even want me to go to work when I left school but when I was 11 my mother got TB and the whole family became chaotic and we really had a fantastic amount of freedom, in fact we were left completely to ourselves, except that I was expected to be mum immediately and take over and cook and do stupid things, and so I haven't had a very conventional sort of life, although my parents are fairly conventional. I mean compared with my brothers, my life became unconventional much earlier than theirs.

NELL I think I mean perhaps the kind of world that you and I move in, the sort of art world, say, for want of a better name. I suddenly feel that – complete lack of security because I don't know how I am meant to behave in any given situation. What I like about working-class girls is that they know how to behave. In any given situation they know how to behave.

PAULINE You see we're thrown into many different situations. I mean we live in a society which is much more classless than any other society in England. Therefore we have to sort of learn how to behave in many different various situations, it terribly varies, we aren't given any particular milieu in which we move where people always react, you know. In fact there's no kind of – there isn't a real tradition about it, you see. For instance one minute you might be going to somewhere where there's a load of smart people and the next moment you're with a lot of artists – you know, it's just sort of like that. And that's probably why one feels like that. But surely one of the sort of things you're saying is that one's trying not to be hypocritical about one's reactions to people and yet in social circumstances most of the manners and things are based on a certain kind of hypocrisy. You know, you smile and shake hands with a person you hate the guts of, and things like that. And this obviously creates a sort of conflict because one is always trying to think 'well I must behave as honestly as I can'.

NELL If you think you should react instinctively, why shouldn't one go and kick someone's teeth in, you know? Is that wrong to go and kick someone's teeth in because they've been out with one's husband or is it right because that's what I would feel like doing?

PAULINE I don't know. You'd obviously hesitate because you wouldn't like your own teeth kicked in.

NELL Yes, that hadn't occurred to me.

PAULINE Well, I like chaos in a way.

NELL You like chaos? Have you ever felt jealous?

PAULINE Yes, I have, but I get jealous over things like if someone has asked me out or something and they spend all their time looking at other girls I kind of feel, 'Well, look, you're spending the evening with me you might as well look at me and I don't care how often you look at pretty girls when you're not with me, but when you're with me you might at least stop doing that! You know, if I looked at other blokes all the time you wouldn't half be sick.'

9

NELL But you've never had that sort of painful, agonising jealousy when one wants to jump out of the window kind of thing?

PAULINE Not really. I don't think so. I suppose again it's to do with possessions again. I don't feel very possessive.

NELL Possessive about your men?

PAULINE No. I feel, 'Well, if they really want to go off, well, it's the best thing.'

NELL Don't you think marriage is out of date?

PAULINE Well, yes. I was rather surprised when I did it but the thing is one is still motivated so much by so many sorts of funny things. Also I thought that if I got married — well, one thinks of difficulties of having children without being married, and unless you've got plenty of money it's a very nasty situation indeed, it can be absolutely awful.

NELL But surely the man's not got any more likely to go — you think he is more likely to go?

PAULINE Oh, I'm talking about if you don't want to live with him.

NELL I see. You mean if you have children and then you decide you don't want to live with him because you get some money for the children kind of thing?

PAULINE Well, I just meant that if you became pregnant — you know, say you were having an affair with someone and you became pregnant and you had the baby, if you don't have any money it's going to be awkward for you and probably the child. Just the physical difficulties of finding a room and you know, when you've got a baby it's terribly difficult.

NELL Would you like to have some children eventually?

PAULINE Well, I suppose so eventually.

NELL But you don't feel the urge now? It interests me because I've wanted to have children since I was about 14.

PAULINE Really?

NELL Yes. I found this art business just got in my way. It just seems to sort of occur . . .

PAULINE I used to vaguely feel that there was something wrong with me because other girls were feeling much more maternal than I was, but in a way I like to find that I don't feel particularly maternal.

NELL It's very good because it leaves you so much freer because this awful feeling clamps one down all the time. One wants babies and then one's got them –

PAULINE I've never really had that you see, and so it hasn't really been a sort of problem for me. I haven't had the feeling of wanting babies.

NELL I wonder if it might suddenly come.

PAULINE Well, it might.

NELL It might never come.

PAULINE Well, I like children you know, but I don't know the sort of feeling that you're describing at all.

NELL Some people seem to think that one is immoral not to have children which is mad because if anything it's the other way round. You don't feel any pressure put upon you?

PAULINE No, not really. At one time I used to get fed up when I went home, this wasn't when I was married or anything, and my father would be playing with his grandson or something and if I held it he'd say, 'that's what I want to see,' and I'd think, 'you silly old fool.' I used to drop it like a hot brick.

NELL I don't completely understand the thing about your getting married.

PAULINE I got married under very extraordinary circumstances, very odd. I mean – I was very heavily involved with someone who was married anyway and really I was getting rather bored with the situation because it was sort of going round in circles, and the whole situation dragged

11

on and on and on and I never really quite believed anything he said, even though probably a lot of it might have
been true, but I never sort of have confidence that people love me. I know people love people at moments you
know, and very genuinely – I can't believe that someone
can love someone consistently, especially if this person's a
bit like me in a way in that I feel a fantastic love for someone, but then the next day I'll be sort of doing something
else and then it might repeat itself but I don't think that a
very strong feeling of love, you know, *that* strong, is just
a smooth thing like that, it sort of goes up and down. It's
like a graph, you know. One of the awful things about
being in a situation of going out with a married man is
that you're kind of sitting in your little box of a room
waiting for a phone call, you know, and for them every
now and again they go up to this box and lift the lid and
take you out and it's lovely, you know, and then they put
you safely back in your box and they go home to children
or something like that, you know. And this kind of situation where you feel . . . and I hate that kind of inactive
thing. I can't stand it, and it just got to a peak when I
thought, 'well, this is just incredibly boring,' and I happened to meet Clive and I wasn't going to marry this man,
I mean I realised that if I lived with him it would last, say,
two years but it may even last longer, I didn't know, you
know. I never expect things to last. But I met Clive about
the time when everything was sort of stewed up and I just
got on terribly well with him, we got stoned all the time
and I only knew him ten days before and he was the very
first man I met who really liked women for one thing – a
terribly rare thing in a man.

NELL It's very rare for men to like women.

PAULINE Yes, I mean it's extraordinary. I mean here was
someone who liked women and to whom they weren't

kind of things, or something you don't quite know about – and because you kind of desire them they're slightly sort of awful, because they bring out the worst in you, this funny sort of puritan idea, sort of Adam and Eve and everything. I mean he was the first man I could really talk very freely to, but I didn't like him at all at first. But he was the first man who made me laugh sort of quite sincerely over the telephone because I'm terrible about the telephone. I don't like the telephone at all.

NELL But I don't see quite why our generation do go on getting married. It seems a bit mad because whenever you want to break, it costs so much money.

PAULINE I still think that people have a thing that by actually marrying someone you're saying something that you can't say in any other way. And as marriage is still very much with society, it really is, that this is the only way that you can sort of say it and even if it's going to break up a year later I don't think it matters all that much because for a while you really said that thing, you know.

NELL And do you feel more secure now you're married?

PAULINE Well, Clive has made me feel much more secure in the way that now I don't mind telling more people about what I think. Because he's given me confidence in the fact that well, perhaps people are interested in the things I want to say, you know.

NELL Does passion mean anything to you?

PAULINE Well, passion always sounds to me like something without any humour in it at all, and I always find humour terribly interesting, and very much a part of life.

NELL I mean that point of being so involved with someone that you're gone. In fact probably a bit like smoking pot only through the sort of ecstasy of love.

PAULINE But then I think that like everything else it's something that zooms up.

NELL I feel that this is the highest point of life, when you're completely gone – I think this is what people feel when they're smoking pot – I mean some people get it through pop music – you're sent.

PAULINE Oh yes, well, I get sent all the time.

NELL But I think by passion I mean being sent through emotional and physical love.

PAULINE But then again, you see it's a thing that lasts for – how long is it going to last? It might last five minutes if you're lucky, an hour if you're luckier still, a day, you know, things like this. I don't think it's terribly important to me because it's so much, say, a part of my life those particular moments. I can remember – I mean this as a passionate moment for me – I can remember once sitting opposite my brother and feeling so much sort of love for him that it was almost as though I was knitted to him, you know. And that lasted for, say, half an hour or something like that and – but I find these things fairly frequent, I've found them less frequent in the last few months only because I've been going through a terrible period of depression and when you get very depressed everything goes along somewhere down there, on a sort of horrible level.

NELL You never get this idea that you're mad to have to get up in the morning and go and act in some stupid play, or it might be a good play you know, that's not the point, it's bloody hard work. Instead of having a marvellous conversation lying by the river or making love to someone?

PAULINE Perhaps I've never loved someone that much. I mean . . . I feel . . . sort of . . . For instance if I felt that with someone I think it's so nice to go off for a while or be me for a while and then come back to it and that makes it much more so for me.

NELL That's true, one can't take that sort of thing all the time.

PAULINE Well, I mean you just cease to feel it.

NELL Do you think sex is tremendously important?

PAULINE Well, it's really important really. It's to do with everything but – and also I think perhaps the kind of sex that's being emphasised at the moment – all around – in books like *The Carpetbaggers* it's the kind that makes me terribly annoyed because it's – oh my God – well it's the usual sort of thing like: 'Her nipples burst free of the restricting brassière into my hand,' sort of practically as though the nipples are gaily laughing and all this kind of, you know, which is sort of stupid and whereas I think sex can be as much – I think sex can be as varied as being alive can be as varied. I think it has all the variations of being alive and feeling and things like that. Sometimes it can be boring, sometimes it can be a joke, sometimes it can be deep intense sort of – you know it can be all those things and I think that one of the terrifying things about the puritanism that still exists in England today is that people are guilty about sex. I think perhaps not so much younger people who are more guilty about violence than anything else and feeling violent.

NELL I think people are extraordinarily guilty about sex, I never have this – I don't know where it comes from.

PAULINE I felt guilty about having an ugly cunt. Oh, I used to think that I had an ugly cunt you see, because when I was very little surrounded by my brothers and everything, who kept yelling, 'shut up, you're only a girl.' I only wanted to be a boy. I used to pull – you know that sort of skin you have – I used to pull it, you see, and I slightly deformed it to make it sort of longer and so I used to spend all my time when I went to bed with someone thinking, 'they'll find out.' But now I've got sort of free and easy about it.

NELL Do things happen to you or do you make them

happen?

PAULINE I'd like to think that I made them happen to me, but I think it's both, you know. I'm very much inclined to sit there and expect things to happen, but somehow things have happened. Clive's always telling me I must stop being like an orphan tossed in the storm. And I do get moments like that when I feel completely dominated with emotional feelings that I just can't control especially with depressions, which is a very worrying thing.

NELL It is an enormous thing. What is one to do about it?

PAULINE I find it one of the most difficult things to control, or to find out ways of stopping. I think that one must do and I must start a plan, I think, and I'll have to because I can get so depressed that it's ridiculous. I've stayed down there far too long and it's got worse as I've got older instead of better.

NELL I think it does.

PAULINE And I think one must fight – instead of sitting there with your depression or lying there crying with your depression, is to really force yourself – and this goes against it – to say get up and do something, even if it's washing up or sweeping the carpet or something like that. But one of the most terrifying things I've found is this thing about going out. But if I've been at home for a particularly long time – if you're painting or anything you can be at home for a long time – to go out becomes terrifying. People are going to look at you on the streets and they're all terrifying. It's extraordinary so I just don't go out.

NELL I've never had that feeling.

PAULINE Oh, it's awful.

NELL When I was young I got depressed but for a very definite reason, whereas now I wake up depressed for no reason at all sometimes.

PAULINE Well, I think you see there probably is a reason which one doesn't really admit to oneself because it's too big a reason somehow. I began getting terrible depressions really after my mother, I mean I began to get these ridiculous depressions apparently without good reason. She's alive, but after she got TB, you know.

NELL She cured it?

PAULINE Yes, she's only got one lung but she's perfectly all right.

NELL And how do you mean you got these depressions after your mother?

PAULINE I might be thinking this wrongly but it seems to me that − I think that up to then my life had been fairly sort of happy in one way, I mean my brothers always tortured me fantastically and in some ways probably − I mean they probably helped to make what I am an awful lot but they used to torture me till I was in such a rage that I would pick up anything to kill them you know, and this was their whole point of doing it, you see, to get me to this point where I was just a screaming maniac, you know. And all sorts of things like this would go on all the time so probably when I was very young, you see, I already had a sort of pattern where I was brought from one sort of very big sort of emotion to another, but I'm sure I didn't get big weepy depressions until I was eleven. But I also got all sorts of things, I got a terrible stammer.

NELL You haven't now much stammer, have you?

PAULINE No, not very much. Sometimes it happens on the telephone or when I'm very nervous or at a certain point with alcohol, I start stammering.

NELL Do you ever get drunk or smoke pot?

PAULINE Oh yes.

NELL Do you like the feeling?

17

PAULINE I like pot the best, I much prefer it to alcohol. And I like being high very much but I find it uses up a lot of nervous energy and leaves me terribly exhausted the day after.

NELL And it can leave you depressed surely?

PAULINE Well, sometimes it can.

NELL What about pills?

PAULINE I've had benzedrine and things but I can't take benzedrine at all because it makes me a complete nervous wreck. Someone closes the door softly and I'm ten feet in the air. But Purple Hearts are better. But I find pills have after-effects.

NELL Have you chosen your men in the past?

PAULINE I've mainly chosen them. But the married man I got involved with literally chose me. It was the first time in my life someone had pursued me so violently, it was a fantastic surprise. He did it from a terribly romantic point of view and he had an extraordinary sort of chemical effect on me. A feeling – he always gave me a sort of fantastic feeling of 'ahuhah', sort of escape, somehow, complete sort of escape and nothing to do with the kind of ordinary things you know. And also he talked in such a romantic language all the time. 'This is fantastic and I've never felt like this' and most people don't – I mean most Englishmen find it very difficult to express themselves in ways like that and to actually hear it spoken is an extraordinary thing. It's slightly frightening as well, you know. You think: 'Oh my God, what are you talking about? This is ridiculous.' And you start being all practical and – I've been fairly lucky in that I'm pretty attractive to men because I have a – quite a sexual sort of quality but along with a thing that's kind of like, oh a happy dumb blonde you see.

NELL How do you have the happy dumb blonde part?

PAULINE But I do have a happy sort of thing and under

certain circumstances I can be extraordinarily dumb!

NELL But that's rather interesting that thing about being pursued because I definitely like the sort of difficult man that just slightly fancies me but I really have to sort of kill myself to . . .

PAULINE Really?

NELL Yes, I don't like people being after me at all. Makes me want to run away.

PAULINE Normally, yes, normally that's absolutely true, yes. Yes, that's quite right because once they start doing it you think: 'Oh you, you just want a quick fuck' or something.

NELL I don't mean that. Not just that actually. I also feel there's some sort of emotional responsibility, that I've got to bother about them.

PAULINE Oh yes, that's true.

NELL They mind if I ring up and say I can't meet them. I feel obliged. I don't want to feel obliged to people.

PAULINE Oh yes, that's awful because you're going to hate them anyway. It's like when you owe people money or they owe you money. When I owe people money every time I see them I'm reminded of it and I grow to hate them – completely unreasonably.

NELL Do you think there's any way we can protect ourselves from sort of getting hard? I mean that if one is living in the world meeting all kind of situations I sometimes feel that the two alternatives are getting hard or having a nervous breakdown.

PAULINE It's terribly difficult. I know it's one of the things about sort of coping isn't it, really and that if – if everything begins to get impossible to cope with because there are so many different levels and all sorts of involvements and things. I think I might have become probably harder in many ways but I'd hate to be hard, that's the very last thing of all. I know I put on hard acts an awful lot, I don't like myself for doing it at all but I find myself in certain situations being all sort of hard and everything almost to cover up the fact that I'm not.

NELL One does that because one is vulnerable.

PAULINE But one knows exactly why one is doing it, it seems so bloody pointless.

NELL It seems to me that there isn't such a thing as a self-confident person because I feel that I've never met one.

PAULINE I know, only people who have the appearance of it. Well, I think everybody's vulnerable always, I mean even if they're only vulnerable on things like their physical appearance and perhaps no other way at all. There always seems to be some point where somebody's vulnerable. I mean the whole idea of hipsterism is not being vulnerable on any of those points, being completely open all the time and not being ashamed of anything you've done or feeling guilty of anything that you are, which I think is a marvellous thing.

NELL Do you think you've got this to a certain extent?

PAULINE To a certain extent but not wholly at all, you know. And whenever I feel things when I suddenly think: 'That's an area where you've got to learn to do something about.'

NELL Do you ever resent the time you spend looking nice?

PAULINE Oh yes, I mean that's one of the difficulties about becoming an actress. What I'd like to do is just put my eyes on in the morning because I always feel that without my eyes I don't exist. But everything else – I just like to wear sort of sloppy things but occasionally be all sort of delicious and very feminine but not half as much as one is supposed to. The fact is that when you dress up mostly you're uncomfortable. And the clothes really aren't as comfortable, are they? They really aren't, you know.

NELL Because one is looking nice one becomes sort of self-aware instead of being aware outwards.

PAULINE Oh yes.

NELL So I resent – I don't want to have to think about myself. I want to think about the sky and the moon and the people across the road. Do you feel strongly about honesty, do you think it's terribly important to say what you really feel?

PAULINE I'd like to be able to say what I really feel but I feel it's impossible, and what you feel is often a paradox – two opposites at the same time sort of thing.

NELL Do you feel you want to be 18 again?

PAULINE No, I'd hate to be 18 again. I'd really hate it, you know. I like growing older.

NELL You never look with dread at the idea of being 40 or 50?

PAULINE I don't look upon 50, funnily enough between 40 and 50 I think it must be hell. No, I have a kind of vague – I can imagine myself being 30 and all through the thirties up to 39 sounds great. What's so extraordinary though is that when one was younger one had an idea that say at 21 when one was very young you were an adult, therefore you were in command of situations, you never had all this faltering feeling and in fact it seems that the areas of non-confidence just change, or new ones develop as more demands are made on you. I wouldn't like to think, 'I think this' and think it forever, things always change, I hope.

NELL Do you get a different sort of kick out of painting and making pictures than you do out of acting?

PAULINE Well, acting can be very egotistical. I think it can be, also it can be very agonising although this didn't occur to me at first, in the way that if you're acting it's you who they're criticising. You know, your actual appearance, your walk, what you're saying, everything, whereas if you're painting, it's just a painting that you've done, it's an object which is somehow set slightly apart from you now that you have done it.

NELL Which do you actually get the most out of doing?

PAULINE Painting. But one of the super things I found when I first started acting was that painting you do alone, you know, and you sit there and it's your own terrible fight or your own lovely bit, whichever sort of phase it's in, but it's really terribly alone and you make the whole thing yourself, the whole construction is, you know – but acting you're part of a team, a lot of people are dependent upon you, you are very dependent upon other people and the conception is the writer's and the director's. The part is something to do with your idea obviously you know, the way you are and everything, but it's part of the something instead of being a thing alone in itself. And therefore you're just part of a whole thing. The responsibilities in that way probably aren't so big but I think the idea of revealing yourself in that particular – you know – just as you are acting this part, is quite a frightening thing. When I first acted and everything it was so much a matter of instinct and for me it has to be quite a lot. I don't know, there are actors who achieve fantastic truth through technical means, a sort of honesty on that stage. Something which they do which becomes a sort of surprise. I think surprise is terribly important anyway. In everything. But acting is also a kind of confidence trick.

NELL What about everyday things like cooking – do you resent the time spent on that?

PAULINE I don't resent it – because I don't spend much time on it and it seems extraordinary that people can have only housework as their only job of life – it would soon kill me off.

June 1965

NELL Now you are pregnant what do you feel?

PAULINE At first I was terrified because I was going to produce something that was part of another person – because you have to accept the fact that you're creating something that is part of them and you're more married to them than you were – and the other big thing – the fear of losing my freedom. But although mentally I didn't like the idea, everything in you works towards you wanting it – I've started becoming obsessive about it – it's taken up a whole great section of my thinking. Also this vanity thing – I'm a very vain person. Before I was pregnant I didn't want a baby, thinking perhaps my tits would sag but now it seems unimportant – all these fears are sliding away. And although it was an accident I'm secretly more pleased about it than I could ever admit.

KATHY

*Twenty-six, has a ten-year-old son
and works in a butter factory*

NELL If you see someone you fancy, how do you go about getting him interested in you?

KATHY Do you mean in a pub or something like that? If he starts asking you if you want a drink you know you're on the firm.

NELL Sometimes do you feel somebody goes on and on at you asking you for a date so that eventually you go?

KATHY It depends really what type of person it is or if you like him. If you know anything about them or anything like that I think it's mostly likely for their ways, not their looks, most probably for their ways because with some people you hear such a lot about them, then when you finally do meet them they're entirely different.

NELL Do you think it's a sort of personal thing in someone, something strikes home to you? You're attracted to them? It goes on from there?

KATHY Yes, definitely. I think so, yes.

NELL What do you think makes you get sick of people?

KATHY Habits – bad habits. Not turning up and that sort of thing. Then again if somebody is sort of set to everything then you can get fed up with them like that. Do you know what I mean? If somebody is sort of perfect you can get fed up with that – they always turn up.

NELL If you inherited a million pounds how would you change your life?

KATHY What would I do with it you mean? I wouldn't stay here anyway. No, I'd like to go to America.

NELL And live out there?

KATHY Mmm.

NELL Would you buy a big place?

KATHY Yes.

NELL And have Yanks?

KATHY No, not really no. I'd just like to, you know, have a big place and everything in it, a swimming pool and all that type of thing.

NELL Don't you think you'd miss Battersea?

KATHY I would yes, I'd like to come back here and that.

NELL Would you take someone with you?

KATHY Most probably, yes. It's quite a lot of money, isn't it?

NELL How would you like the place done out?

KATHY Nothing special really, you know, like modern. Like people have places in Battersea, nothing fantastic, you know what I mean?

NELL You wouldn't have it fantastic?

KATHY No, not really. Just ordinary really.

NELL In Battersea no one's got a swimming pool.

KATHY Not in Battersea no, but sort of round here they have now, haven't they? Mind you there is moneyed people in Battersea. Like down Battersea Park Road, round there, the Mansions and that type of thing. A lot of stars live down there. Yes, quite a lot of stars live down there.

NELL So you'd have a big place in New York or some-where? In the city or in the country?

KATHY No, I've not all that time for that. Because, well, you don't really know because if you come into that much money you don't really know what you'd do with it, do you? You sort of dream about it don't you, you know, if you win the pools or something like that, what you'd do, but most probably you'd do entirely different things.

NELL What's the minimum you'd think you need a week to live comfortably?

KATHY For a married couple? I think a man's got to earn at least £25. First of all it's £5 rent anyway. That's if just one of you are at work. You could live comfortably on £25. I think. By the time you've paid your rent, and say £10 for the housekeeping and the rent's paid, that still leaves him with £10 doesn't it? For a car or something – it's two or three quid a week isn't it for a car? A lot of men don't earn that money do they?

NELL But what do you think is the least a family can manage on? Man and wife and a couple of kids?

KATHY £10.

NELL Do you think that's very hard?

KATHY Definitely. It's why you find yourself getting in debt. People have to borrow.

NELL There seems quite a lot of money about to me. For instance, I go into a shop to buy the baby a pair of shoes and I'll buy him one pair of shoes and when they're worn out I buy him another. Whereas I saw a woman, she was just a working-class woman, with a kid, buying a couple of pairs of shoes, a pair of slippers, for a kid of two years old. It wouldn't need all that. So there seems to be a lot of money about.

KATHY Yes, but then really you find that type of person as a rule hasn't got a lot of money, they're that type of person who would buy two or three pairs of shoes. With a person who has got money and as you say when they're worn out they buy another pair. You see most probably buying two pairs of shoes, that kid might grow out of them, they might not even fit him, but they do have that type of thing. Same as if I buy Mike anything if I've got the money – tomorrow it's gone, that's how you think, as long as they've got something, the kids. Like I might buy two or three shirts. Because tomorrow he won't have it. It's gone, hasn't it? He'll most probably find himself spending it on something else and you say, 'I wish I'd bought him that' – you know what I mean?

NELL But do you find that when you have money that you don't really plan very much how you spend it?

KATHY Not really, except for the things I've got to pay. I give my mum her money and then the things I've got to pay like clubs, or something like that.

NELL You put that aside. And the rest of the money you just spend?

KATHY Yes, I just spend it.

NELL So you might equally well if you saw a nice jumper buy that? Or you might equally well spend it all in the pub buying people drinks?

KATHY I might, yes.

NELL Which is very good, because another thing I find about people who haven't got a lot of money, they're often quite generous.

KATHY They are, they are very generous, yes. They live for today, that's the point.

NELL Do you think that's really the best way to live, to live for today?

KATHY Well I think so, you never know what's going to happen tomorrow, do you? You don't really, do you? I mean lots of people they plan and they put this away for when they get old and that type of thing and then anything happens and who has it, their kids, don't they? I think while you've got it, spend it. You haven't got it tomorrow. I think so myself, because I often find that I've been out with a couple of quid and maybe somebody in a pub – and I couldn't get one person a drink and not – say there's a crowd of them. I'd have to make a call for the whole lot and then it's gone. That's all there is to it, it's gone hasn't it?

NELL I think one of the things about you is you're not frightened of hard work, are you, it doesn't worry you?

KATHY No, that's the way really we've been brought up.

NELL You've always worked?

KATHY Well, my mum's sort of had to go to work, you know, and keep us when we were kids, when it was hard. They reckon years ago that the times – I mean things didn't cost a lot of money and all that type of thing and they didn't get as much money anyway. It's just the same today, things are dearer and the money's gone up. And we've had to look after ourselves and then you find that when the time does come that you've got to go to work you don't really mind. Whereas a person who has had everything and then when the time comes that they haven't got it they find it hard, don't they, to go to work? I think so anyway.

NELL Does the idea of being old worry you?

KATHY Not at all.

NELL What about losing your looks? Because now you can walk into a pub and get pretty well any man.

KATHY No, it doesn't bother me, I never think about it. No, it's funny isn't it? It never bothers me. Lots of people say that.

NELL That's another thing, you'll probably be just as capable of having a good time then as you are now.

KATHY It all depends I think what type of person you are. If you are very busy and don't mix with people and you don't get on with people and if you're the other way inclined you'll always be like that. They say you change but I don't think you do. I don't think so at all. If you're going to get on with people, I mean people like me, I – if I went out with anybody and I met anyone I find I always get on with people. I don't very often say, 'Well I don't like them', unless they're entirely different to me and they – you find some people they disagree with everything you say, they go the opposite way to you but I find I get on with most people really.

NELL Did you find that when you were about 15 you had a sort of idea of what life would be like? And it's turned out very different to what you thought?

KATHY Yes.

NELL What did you think it was going to be like when you were about 15?

KATHY Well, when you're 15 you think about getting a fellow and getting married. Fifteen you're just starting work, aren't you, and everything's sort of all new and different and then you get out and about, find yourself a fellow and you think it's all going to change, you're going to get married and have a place and all that type of thing.

NELL It's going to be very romantic?

KATHY And it isn't. For one thing you can't get a place if you wanted to get married, can you? That's the whole thing really. That's a lot of the trouble really, isn't it? Can't get a place. People with five and six kids in one room. There are people who are lucky to find places but I don't think people ought to get married anyway when they're young.

NELL Do you think people should get married at all or do you think it's an out-of-date idea?

KATHY I think it's everyone to their own belief really. If people want to get married, people think they've got to get married really, don't they? Young girls, I mean it's every young girl's wish to get married, isn't it? And then I think if people want to live with somebody, I think lots of people get on far better. I mean I know several people that have lived with somebody for years, maybe they've been married and it sort of broke up and they live with somebody and they get on entirely better. I think so, yes. I have heard quite a few people that I know of and they're really happy.

NELL Would you ever get married again?

KATHY I don't know really. It's such a long time ago. I don't think of myself as ever being married really.

NELL Don't you?

KATHY No. I was so young and then I didn't have any responsibility really.

NELL How old were you when you were married?

KATHY 16.

NELL And you stopped being married when you were how old?

KATHY 22. The thing is, it's alright if you're young and you've got a place, that's the whole thing, if you've got a flat then you know you've got responsibilities but if you live at home . . .

NELL You never left your mum?

KATHY No. If you live at home and then you've got your mother and all that, you know . . .

NELL It's just the same as having your boyfriend in for the night?

KATHY Of course it is, it's just the same isn't it? Whereas if you've got a flat of your own you go and work and you can buy things, whereas if you're at home and you've got one room, what can you buy really? Whereas if you've got a flat, that is the whole thing of getting married, you go out to work and buy something every week and that is the whole point of it really, isn't it?

NELL When you've got a nice place going?

KATHY Yes. Whereas if you live with your mother you haven't got any chance at all really.

NELL Do you think life is very hard?

KATHY Yes, definitely.

NELL In what way?

KATHY Well in every way I think so. I'm not sad about going to work because I don't mind working. I'd rather go to work than be home all day. Unless like maybe if I had young children. But I think you can find that by being home all day you get bored, whereas if you go to work it does take it off a bit. And you've got something to come home to and all that. But what is there really anyway in life? It's the same thing day after day, isn't it?

NELL What does one live for?

KATHY I don't know. Not yourself, that's obvious. Unless you've got kids, maybe your kids, you live for. But it is the same thing, you go and have a drink, you go to the pictures, it is the same thing day after day.

NELL Even if you've got kids, it's the same thing, you wash them and clean them and get them up.

KATHY You get them out to school in the morning, same thing, isn't it? I think it is hard, I mean it should be entirely different I think.

NELL But you could never imagine committing suicide for instance?

KATHY I could imagine committing suicide, yes.

NELL In what moments have you thought of it?

KATHY Oh you know, something – I've really been upset about something and I have really thought of doing it, yes.

NELL How would you do it then?

KATHY I thought about gassing myself.

NELL It'd cost you two or three bob in the meter.

KATHY Mind you, it does need a lot. When you think of it again, it does need a hell of a lot of nerve.

NELL Do you think you know what's going to happen in the next world?

KATHY No. I don't know whether I really think there is anything – another world. Do you?

NELL No, I don't. Are you frightened of dying?

KATHY No.

NELL Why not?

KATHY Well, that's the whole thing, you don't know what's going to happen to you. If you did know – I mean no one will ever be able to tell you that, will they? If you did know, I think it would be more frightening then. You could be anywhere, you could be in the street for instance, you could drop dead, nothing – you wouldn't know anything about it would you?

NELL No, but you do know if you're ill and you die slowly.

KATHY Oh yes, that's a terrible thing, I wouldn't like that. I'd rather be given something and that's it, wouldn't you?

NELL Yes, I would.

KATHY I mean to go into hospital like a lot of people – you do find it in young people, people what's got cancer and things like that. The point is, if I was ill and I had something wrong with me like I was in terrible pain or something like that, or had an idea that I had cancer – people don't accept it do they? And I think if it was me and I went into hospital I'd think straight away, you know, 'You've got something wrong with you, you're very ill' and you know yourself that you're not going to get over it, I mean there is times that I have been ill and I've been in hospital and you think to yourself, 'Well I'm not going to get over this.'

NELL I've never thought that I was going to die in hospital. Have you?

KATHY Yes. I have – I was in hospital – and then you go down and you have a pre-med and you never think you're coming back. I have, quite often have I thought of that yes. Whereas I can't make that out where people don't know, you know what I mean? Like say somebody's who's been talking about this, like say somebody's died with it in their family, died with an illness, any sort of illness, and then they're taken ill and they go into hospital, well they won't accept the fact that they're going to die. They won't accept that. If it was me and I went into hospital and I was very ill and I knew that, I would accept that fact, I would have to ask. I would have to find out.

NELL Do you find that most people are frightened of death?

KATHY Most people are, yes.

NELL People don't discuss it very much do they?

KATHY No they don't. And I find that people – a very funny thing about – you know, somebody – they might not like somebody like say, somebody down the street they live in, for instance, and they're always sort of talking about that person, they don't like them and all their bad faults and everything like that, and then when they die, that's what makes me laugh – when they die they have the cheek to turn around and say, 'Oh what a nice person!' Or 'Oh, he was a lovely man!' Don't they though? I was talking about that to somebody the other day.

NELL They don't like to put bad words on the dead, is it?

KATHY You'll find that out later on, but they should turn around and say, 'Oh I didn't like him'; I think that they should say that, be straight and say it. But they don't, they say, 'Oh well he's a nice fellow' and that and maybe a week before they were just giving him a bad name. That's

34

the type of people there is and I think everyone should leave everyone alone to lead their own sort of life, I think so. You find that if people didn't interfere and –

NELL This is terribly true – people ruin each other's lives, make them miserable. Particularly in a place which is very close together like Battersea for instance, where you really can't do anything without everyone knowing, can you?

KATHY Course you can't, no.

NELL Does it worry you at all what people think of you?
KATHY No.

NELL You're very good about that, you really don't care do you?

KATHY Well, I think while they're talking about you they're leaving somebody else alone and what can talk do anyway? What can it do?

NELL Upset you.

KATHY Well it can upset you, yes, but you get over it, don't you? Whereas if you know, most probably if you know it's the truth, and then it hurts you, but people just gossip don't they? If you know that's not the truth you don't bother, you can walk past with your head up, that's what I think. It does hurt you, I must admit, it does hurt you when someone says something about you and it is the truth.

NELL But do you hear a lot of things that have been said about you at various times?

KATHY Not much really, no. Most probably people do and you don't even hear about it. I don't think I really ever have. I find that I sort of get on with people and – like my friends for instance, I always keep a friend. I don't have one for maybe six months, I like to have a friend for a long time, I've got a friend who's a friend for life, really a true friend, you've got a friend for life, you know what

I mean?

NELL Do you ever fall out with Jean?

KATHY No, I never have since when we were kids.

NELL For instance, when I was living in Lavender Road, you didn't seem to see so much of Jean then. She was just married, I suppose?

KATHY She was just married, yes. And then I didn't see a lot of her. She used to be out and about.

NELL Was she very smart when she was out? I should imagine she was.

KATHY She was, she was very smart, yes. He used to play in the band, and he used to take her everywhere and everywhere he went she used to go with him and that type of thing. Playing in the band that's the worst thing you can have really. They were very close, you know, it's very hard to believe really. And then all of a sudden they start getting out with their mates one night a week, and then it's two nights.

NELL But what do they do, I mean what's the point of going out with boys, as it were, what do they do?

KATHY They go out and have – some men they just go out and have a good drink. Some men come home and give their money and they're nice as anything and the next minute they might be out with somebody else. That's the whole point.

NELL What do you think of the meaning of that expression 'having a good time' – what does 'having a good time' mean to you?

KATHY Well, going to parties and that sort of thing, mixing with people. Different people. Mostly all your friends, but then when you go to parties, there always is somebody different there. I like parties or going swimming and that sort of thing, sport, really. I get a lot of fun out of that, going out for the day and going swimming you know, a crowd of you, and having a drink and that type of thing.

NELL You prefer that really to a quiet life? A place and being in each night.

KATHY Really, yes.

NELL That wouldn't suit you?

KATHY No. I did have a go at that.

NELL How long did you have a go at that for?

KATHY Six years. Most probably if you'd got the right type of person, you think enough of a person – there is a time that you do find somebody. Like somebody said to me like, somebody was married, just got married because all his mates were getting married and he was on his own. All his mates got married and it sort of left him, you know? So the first girl, you know, a nice girl he got to taking out, he got married, not because he was in love with the girl or anything like that and he just used to say to himself, 'Well, if I ever found somebody that I really fancy, I really, I was really in love with, I'd be gone and that would just be the end of it.' You know, you go on and on looking for somebody.

NELL Do you think people don't have much sort of respect for marriage now?

KATHY No, they don't. Like years ago. Like my mum – you hear them talking about years ago.

NELL Your husband was your husband and that was it.

KATHY That was it, yes. You were married and you were married.

NELL You mean people didn't carry on much then?

KATHY Well, they did carry on but you didn't hear as much of it then as what you do now. As for lesbians, my mum never heard of anything like that. Like just lately, you know? My mum never knew what it was.

NELL Is there a lot about just lately, lesbians?

KATHY Oh, there is more, yes. Definitely. I mean everywhere you go.

NELL Do you see lesbians in Battersea?

KATHY Oh yes. There's lots in Battersea now. What about the girl who was in the pub and you said you'd like to sketch her one night, she was singing on the mike, that girl who was a prostitute. What about her? I mean she's married, got two kids, she's been married twice, got two kids, she was on the game and she's turned lesbian. Who'd ever believe that? I was out the other night somewhere, I was sitting in the pictures and I was shocked, she was sitting down in front of me, kissing and cuddling with this –

NELL With a girl?

KATHY Yes. She could have been no more than 20. Very, very timid looking thing and she's a great big sort isn't she?

NELL Isn't it amazing? They could get arrested, could they?

KATHY They can't apparently.

NELL Can't they?

KATHY No. She was in the show and everything, in the Cricketers.

NELL They can kiss and cuddle with a girl and not get arrested? I didn't know that. I thought it was illegal.

KATHY Lots of people don't know, do they, that they're girls, do they?

NELL They're dressed like men?

KATHY She dresses like a man and everything, you know.

NELL Or could you see straight away that she's a woman?

KATHY I could, I could myself, I mean lots of people might not, some people are very stupid, like my mum for instance, you know what I mean? Or my dad like, we were in a pub and my dad didn't even know that somebody was like it. My dad didn't believe it, they're old-fashioned really, you see they didn't see it going on much in their time and expect it's still the same. That's the thing.

NELL Do you think people are born queers or lesbians or do they just turn that way from bad influence?

KATHY I think some are. Some of it is born in them I think. Or some of them – with men – I think it's a lot to do with their mothers, for instance the only child – you don't often find that – that it is the only child, it might be a big family, I know there's a big family of 12 kids and one of the roughest, one of the roughest fellows that you could ever wish to meet and he got three years' imprisonment and I was out one night and this queer kept looking on, we were having a drink and this queer kept sort of looking and I was shocked, I saw this fellow there, we'd been friends since we was kids and he'd been in prison and anyway he had to leave. This queer who he was with made him leave the pub because he kept looking at him. I was never so shocked in my life to see him like it.

NELL How extraordinary, Kath. You can't trust anyone.

KATHY They can't help it, I think they should be left alone, it's their life.

NELL Do you? It doesn't matter?

KATHY It's disgusting to us, really, but if they don't interfere with anyone then why not let them get on with it? Same as man and wife are probably disgusting to them. I think they should be left alone, let them do what they like.

NELL Yes, a private thing.

KATHY Well, it is, yes. People think they're in love with a man – well, it's entirely up to them, which they do believe don't they? It's just like husband and wife or girl and boy, that's how they act towards each other, don't they though?

NELL What do you think is the most important thing in life?

KATHY Money. Money, yes. There is a lot of things you can do with money.

NELL Like what sort of things? Once you've got a place.

KATHY Buy things and there's a hell of a lot that people can do with money what people can't who haven't got it. The most important thing I think is for two people to be happy really, with each other, I think that's the most important thing. If you do find someone you can be really happy with, because you do find even if you haven't got – as I said before – if you haven't got anything you find that you can be happy with a person, if you haven't got two halfpennies really. Whereas some people they've got everything and they're not happy at all, they look for happiness elsewhere. I think so.

NELL Finally, if you've got everything what is there left for you to buy? So what can you do?

KATHY That's the whole point.

NELL And you see these rich women down the West End, you know just sour old bitches with the smartest clothes on, what good does it do them?

KATHY Nothing at all. They might as well go about in rags and be happy.

NELL That's true, they can't get lovers, no one wants them. Probably don't have any sex.

KATHY No. You could probably find a person who hasn't got anything. They haven't got any clothes or anything like that, but you could find that some people would really fancy them, be in love with them, and they haven't got anything at all. You do find that yes.

NELL What age do you think a man's at his best?

KATHY 25 to 30.

NELL And a woman?

KATHY 25, 26.

NELL I think it's quite true this, because one's at one's prime of life.

KATHY When you get near thirty.

NELL You're at your best?

KATHY Yes. Towards thirtyish.

NELL Because you know everything and you're still young.

KATHY Yes, you know everything. That's true, yes. If you have kids, I think that's a good thing as well.

NELL But you don't think life might be sort of empty when you're about 45?

KATHY Not really, no. It all depends what type of partner you've got really. Like for instance Jean's mum and dad. She's got a grown-up family, they're all married and Jean's mum is sixty but they go out, and have a drink and they're a really happy couple.

NELL And is her mum nice?

KATHY She is, very attractive. You wouldn't think her mum was sixty, to have a grown-up family. She doesn't come out a lot during the day but they sort of please their-self what they do. They might go out to a celebrity club over the West End, have a meal, and have a show, you know, and please theirself, you know.

NELL Have they got a nice place?

KATHY Very lovely place they've got. They've got everything. Very devoted. They're a close family. Now they're all grown-up and they're married and they're very close to their mother. They're all for their mother and father.

NELL Do you think you've made any big mistakes in the past?

KATHY Definitely.

NELL Like what?

KATHY Getting married when I was 16.

NELL You should just never have got married?

KATHY No.

NELL What could you have done, said to your mum, 'I just don't want to get married'?

KATHY Mum didn't want me to get married.

NELL Well, why did you then?

KATHY Well, you just think you're having a baby and that's the whole thing really. The point is, you don't get married anyway really unless you're really mad at 16, unless you're expecting a baby, really. And then you've got to think about the baby and by then, well, you are sort of a baby yourself and then when something like that happens – overnight you're grown-up. You are sort of grown-up and you realise that you've got to think about the baby you just don't have to think about yourself any more, you're sort of out having a good time and all that sort of thing until it does happen, you always think it can't happen to you. You always think that. You think, 'oh, so and so's expecting a baby' and how silly that was and you don't realise and it does finally happen to you.

NELL Did you feel terrible when you were having the baby? Worried and everything?

KATHY Not really, because I find that you get a lot of advice, especially when you are young. Years ago, people did have children young, lots of people, but girls now they get married when they're 18, 20. That's not too bad but when you're 16 –

NELL That's very young.

KATHY And it doesn't matter what people tell you. People tell you all sorts of things but you don't really know what's going to happen. Like if it's your first baby people say you know, this was terrible in labour and all this type of thing which I don't think they should tell you that, it does frighten you, really everyone's frightened, I think so. But you don't know what's going to happen yourself, you've got to sort of experience that, you don't really know what you are going through. Then when you do go through it, you find it's entirely different to what people tell you.

NELL But did you think it was a terrific experience?

KATHY Yes, I did. It's really marvellous really, having a baby.

NELL Were you thrilled about it even then, being so young?

KATHY Oh, yes. I was.

NELL What did you feel when you first saw Michael?

KATHY I don't know. It just seemed impossible really. It does. It really seems impossible, you don't think that it is you that's had it, you know what I mean? Really marvellous. Specially if you're feeling alright in yourself and everything. Some people have bad confinements and others are quite alright. Specially when you're young and you don't think it really is you who's had a baby really. Someone says, 'you've got a lovely son' and you look around to see who they're talking to. I find when I look back you can't explain it really. I don't think so, to anyone. It's very hard to put it down you know, you wanted to write about it. It's just a feeling you've got and it's very hard to tell anybody else about it. It's really a marvellous feeling to have a baby, but it's very hard to explain it to anybody else when you think about it. Even then, you know you think to yourself the mistakes you've made and all that but when you look back on it I think it's marvellous. You forget. At the time I, even then I thought to myself, 'what a mistake I've made getting married', at the time when I had Michael you sort of forget all about that and think to yourself you're going to try and a make a go of it. When you've got a baby you try and be nice and that type of thing. Make a go of it and make it last. You find it doesn't work out like that always, does it?

NELL Do you think you can, if things are really bad, do you think effort alone can make a marriage work?

KATHY Sometimes. Sometimes it can. I think the best thing to do, if you've enough guts, if you do feel like that, towards somebody, you think you've made a mistake, if you've got enough guts and you've got somewhere to go, I think the best thing to do is get out. I think so myself. But you find that's not always possible. Lots of people won't take you in with a kid, you've got to go to work to keep them anyway. But if you can find somebody or somebody to look after them, I think that's the best thing to do, that is. Because it's only spoiling both your lives the longer it goes on, where one person thinks a hell of a lot of the other person and the other one's got no feelings at all, you're just spoiling both your lives really. You should if you can get out. It's hard; it's easy for people to talk about it, but you do find it is impossible because – for instance where money – if you've got money you can. Whereas if you've got nothing with a kid, you do find it very hard. Whereas if you've got money, it doesn't matter who it is, if you've got money, people will take you in. Give them a few quid and everything's quiet really.

NELL But how important do you think sex is in a relationship between people?

KATHY I think it's the most important thing, really. Myself, really. Well, that is the whole point, that is the whole part of it, really.

NELL Do you think a lot of marriages and things break up because it's no good?

KATHY Yes, definitely. You find men going somewhere else, picking up something else. Just for sex. They might be happy in the home and all that type of thing. 'Well, I love my wife' as I say, come home and give them wages every week and that type of thing, you know, whereas they go elsewhere to find sex because . . .

NELL And that's no good because the wife isn't happy?

KATHY Course not. I think that is the main, really the main part in a marriage, is sex. With anyone, if you're living with a person, that's the most important part, yes.

NELL But your marriage didn't really break up because of sex did it?

KATHY Well, no not really. In a way it did, yes, because I didn't like sex at all. It was alright first of all, I was sort of courting and when I think I had Michael really I found that I didn't like sex any more. I sort of felt it was disgusting. That was the whole thing really. No man is going to stand that. The point is they're just not – just, 'I've married someone just so that – just for sex?' I mean your whole life's not based on that, but it is a most important part. I think really if you enjoy sex it does help a lot.

NELL And how long did it take you to get back into the way of enjoying it again?

KATHY I didn't.

NELL How long?

KATHY Well, I never did any more.

NELL What, till he left you?

KATHY Mmm. I never did.

NELL And then meeting someone new it started all over again, it was all right?

KATHY Only different. It was entirely different. It was a different type of thing.

NELL How strange.

KATHY It really is, isn't it, when you think of it?

NELL Maybe you grew up somehow?

KATHY Maybe that's what it was, maybe I was young.

When you're going out and about it's all sort of a new thing isn't it?

NELL He never suited you anyway?

KATHY Not really, no. I mean he was quite nice looking and all that, I mean young girls went for that type of thing didn't they? He was a nice-looking fellow. 'You're very lucky, he's handsome-looking.' Really, it was nice to be seen about. You know, and I used to go everywhere, like, where I'd never been before. My mother was really strict with us when we were kids, we had to be in by 9 o'clock and all that sort of thing, you know, and then you find you meet somebody when you leave school and it starts off a new life really. You leave school and then you are allowed to stay up a bit longer and all that. You find yourself taking liberties. You meet somebody and you think it's all quite a new thing really, going out and you go out to a pub and have a drink and you think it's really good. It's not really, you know. Sometimes really if you listened to your parents – sometimes, it doesn't matter what they say to you, it doesn't help at all, because you're entirely different and no one will ever change that. Not only your mother and father, no one will change what you think if you do – if I did listen to my mother I might have found myself in a different position to what I am. If I hadn't have got married. I mean I still could have – I could have, could I?

NELL Yes, you'd have saved a lot of time.

KATHY Yes, quite a few years of your life are wasted really, when you look back.

NELL But now when you meet someone you think a lot of – you know, you think something of, sex is very important to you?

KATHY It is important, yes.

NELL And you think it's very important to a man, it

keeps a man?

KATHY Yes. Certainly. Not with some men. I mean some men – with some women – some women you hear them say it doesn't bother them and all that type of thing and the same with some men. It all depends what kind of nature you are, I think. With some men, you know, they're married to someone, they're very good, I mean they might be the most horriblest person you've ever met, ugly and things like that, and he's very handsome. You often find a really handsome man – I know someone who's like that and she's a right horror, you know what I mean? But she's very good where sex is concerned, very good in bed.

NELL Really. That's a thing that always interests me, because you think someone can really be good in bed whoever they're with, don't you think it just depends if two people meet who are good with each other? Or do you think there can be one woman who's good with whatever man she goes with? And a man who can be really good with whatever woman he goes with?

KATHY No. I don't think so. Well, I don't know. With a lot of men they just don't bother, they don't care what it is. They don't. A lot of men don't care what – I mean I've heard it said a lot of men don't care what it is as long as it's sex. As long as it's there. A few think entirely different, they wouldn't do that type of thing. But I think it all depends what type of person they are, what man and what woman it is really. With a woman if it's a – some women I think they do use sex to get somebody. Just for that reason. They're very good at it and very good in bed and they sort of can keep a person like that, I think so.

NELL You think you can?

KATHY I think you can if you're very good at sex, you know. I'll say no more.

FRANCES

Died in 1964, at 27; she left two daughters

ENCOUNTER
Why are you so silent?
Don't you remember my name?
Before our mouths met
On a thread of lust
I had only seen:
Stiff black hairs on your wrists
And a tear in your hip pocket
That I wanted to mend

NELL Do you think people's lives are hindered by conventions?

FRANCES Emotional life isn't so determined by conventions, it's pretty natural. If you listen closely to what's going on inside you and you usually do if it's important to you, when something's urging you to do something and you don't know why – if you listen quietly you find out.

NELL Do you think marriage is out of date?

FRANCES I'm in a complete muddle about it at the moment. I only know I definitely don't want it. My motives are so confused. I don't want to hinder my man in any way. I want to leave him free for anything he might prefer later

on. If only there were some way without being aggressive women could retain their own identity while making
men happy. I don't see any reason why it's incompatible
with marriage but it's so rare that I resist marrying again.
I don't want to be safe. I like to feel I'm in control of my
life. I don't know how far I'm fooling myself.

NELL How do you deal with everyday chores?

FRANCES I work while the children are at school but I
do find I work much better later and later and that's rather
difficult to combine with one's ordinary life. I can't separate my responses, I'm body and spirit. I want the house
to be clean, people are hungry and need feeding or children need looking after. Scrubbing a floor isn't so different
from sitting down and writing a poem. All my actions are
responses to some demand. I'm there to satisfy them.

NELL Does the word passion mean anything to you?

FRANCES Yes, goodness me, yes. What kind of passion
do you want to talk about?

NELL On the sort of love level. Ecstasy — what it's all
about — does it make everything seem dim beside it? If
you could live in a state of constant passion, would you?

FRANCES I can't understand how anyone could want
to. If you didn't have a certain amount of time scrubbing
floors — I don't see that one should regret having to scrub
floors and scrub potatoes — they are simply the sort of
things that make the other ecstasy possible.

NELL Do you know the difference between right and
wrong?

FRANCES I'm still conditioned by what I was taught as
a child however much I may rebel. I know immediately
something's wrong like adultery. You can't avoid — not a
feeling of guilt — but an awareness of what other people
think of it.

NELL I think the thing about strict moral codes is that

there is a definite rule, but don't you feel that we have a different response for everything? That we look at the situation and then decide whether it's right or wrong?

FRANCES Yes, I think all intelligent people should do that with every situation on every level. But one isn't capable of that continual effort so one acts instinctively on a mixture of tribal code and desire. Some men don't like the direct approach at all. I had a boy once, it was disastrous. We were absolutely mad about each other. It was just no good because I said, 'You're marvellous I'd like to go to bed with you,' and he thought about it and then he said 'It's no good I can't take the direct approach, I'm used to seducing women!' It put him off for a whole week!

NELL Is sexual fidelity a hypocrisy that just doesn't work?

FRANCES I've thought about it so much. There seem very few practical reasons for sexual fidelity in marriage – now there's no danger of putting a cuckoo in the nest. And more than that, it's a cumulative thing when the old laws break down, of people wishing to be independent, seeking desperately for their new identity. How far can you make any promises anymore? How can you make it possible for there not to be an awful amount of mud-slinging after a few years – 'you never told me this is the sort of thing you would want to do, expect to do.' I think one has to be completely honest inasfar as it is possible because you don't even know what your own motives are half the time, but as far as you can genuinely be honest with the man you love, tell him what you think your needs are. It's rather like the system in America where you estimate your income tax for the next year, saying what you think your earning capacity's likely to be, what kind of direction you think you're going in, and trying to be as honest as possible in paying your dues.

51

NELL Did you like American women?

FRANCES I can't think of any I feel really close to, no. Because they appear not to be spontaneous. I may be completely wrong about it, I don't know that many, and I certainly know none closely. But they're not spontaneous with their men, which may be a good thing or a bad thing but therefore I find it difficult to talk to them about men. They do appear always to be looking for what they can get back out of a relationship, not financially but emotionally: the whole relationship's measured by this. It's rare to find anyone who is willing to give and go on giving and not keep counting what's coming in, which I think is the whole trouble with all relationships. They never work once you start demanding, never. I'm not being idealistic because I know that people do this all the time. Immediately they feel insecure in any way they demand something to compensate. A girl who's unhappy goes out and buys a new dress, and immediately forgets her broken heart. A man does the same thing, buys a new motorbike, a car, a leather belt, a pair of boots and it's an extremely human weakness that when you feel a draught you want to stuff something in it. American women seem to me to do this the whole time.

NELL Tell me about jealousy. You've felt jealous have you?

FRANCES Yes. Often. But we were talking about feeling more confident and certainly a bit clearer by now, our mid-twenties, about what one wants to do, having been through a gargantuan effort to decide and then reconcile it with being a woman. It is rather like being a negro and having to get over the whole problem of being black before you can write about anything else – it's exactly like that. If you feel, as one is brought up to feel, a second-class citizen, inferior to a man in every way, encouraged to think of oneself as the object of a man's pursuit and therefore with no vital life of your own except to be buffers for the train. But having got through that, having discovered that there were other things I wanted to do, discovered what they were, attempted to do them and feeling I've got a foothold anyway, jealousy doesn't seem to affect me in the same way. I'm a person in my own right, I can cause jealousy, I'm not waiting to be jealous – I'm not in a susceptible position any more. I'm jealous because it's a completely reflex action, that if you see a pretty girl going up to your man and he shows interest in her or you hear of something he's doing or in any way one feels his lack of interest temporarily, however temporarily, in you. One doesn't expect to be the prime mover in his life, but one feels jealous nonetheless. Everything else tells you to be sensible and to relax and it makes it much easier to bear.

NELL But you've never done anything to another woman in revenge?

FRANCES No.

NELL And you can't imagine kicking someone's teeth in?

FRANCES Oh yes, I can. Certainly I can. I've never had to do it thank God. My goodness yes, I'd fight, I really would, if I thought someone was trying to get my man from me.

NELL Can you describe what it's like being in love?

FRANCES It's total response of one's whole person. One can't describe it in an image because it's absolutely life itself. Almost as though one is an extremely sensitive lens, it's as though one can suddenly see, having thought one could see for the whole of one's life and suddenly finding one had been living in the dusk land.

NELL Can you manage with more than one man in your life at a time?

53

FRANCES On a very primitive basis, I can only *love* one man at a time. If I have any other men – and then I only have them when I'm away from the person I'm in love with – that's usually not purely for sex, but a combination of missing the person I'm in love with and a feeling of freedom and a good time to experiment and discover about other people and I find in that time I'm extremely responsive to other people, much more than I've ever been in periods when I've not been in love with someone. It's quite extraordinary. I have the most marvellous communication – it sounds terribly corny – but simply being free of any kind of need of them in fact, being able to be completely objective about them and not needing them for myself, in any way, it was absolutely marvellous, with no barriers, no bad things at all. Quite extraordinary – all kinds of different people, I mean none of them the same as each other. In another way I think of being in love as rather like a ship that's full of treasure and everybody seems to know it's there and want to have a bit of it and touch it or taste it in some way and you do notice the effect on other people, tremendously. And for me, if I'm on my own, other people know I'm in love with someone else but it doesn't hinder them in the slightest wanting to be interested in me.

NELL How can one achieve a balance between being so emotionally sensitive and in constant danger of nervous breakdown and alternatively being so tough life becomes meaningless?

FRANCES I've never discovered it. I live in hope that I shall find a happy compromise but I have never discovered it. In a way you can't expect to have nerve endings without their being painful. If you're not going to respond to things, the good and the bad, the painful and the ecstatic, you'll be metaphorically living in the suburbs in a four-roomed house, scrubbing your Aga with a piece of wire wool. I can't do it, I try to protect myself against the worst things that can happen to me, but very amateurishly.

NELL About the idea of losing your looks. Do you feel in some way you'll lose your power?

FRANCES It used to bother me when I was 15 or 16. I think when you're an adolescent you keep writing off panic-stricken for the latest face cream because of dreadful things in women's magazines, making it appear that the whole point of a woman's life is the time when she's attractive to a man, which isn't a logical argument to me at all. That's just a part of one's life. It's not all a woman can do, it's not all that she, I'm sure, wants to do. I want to feel myself a human being first and a woman second.

NELL Can you imagine yourself when you're much older, say between fifty and sixty?

FRANCES I hope I shall be wiser, more relaxed with people, able to communicate a bit better – things I'm trying to do now, painfully. I hope I shall have succeeded.

NELL I look forward to being older, as a release from tension.

FRANCES I don't want to get rid of the tension but I simply want to get rid of all the things in myself which I criticise. It's a continual battle, moving forward slowly and I'm fighting every inch of the way to learn anything, to be able to do anything. Each little experiment and battle takes you only an inch up the road as it were. I can't see myself being very far up the road by the time I'm fifty or sixty, but surely I'll be some distance along.

EDNA

Thirty-two; has two sons and has published four novels

NELL One of the things I wanted to ask you about was the thing of being a writer and having children. One of the most difficult things is, apart from the practical thing of having the time, there's also the emotional thing of having time to sort of sink down into yourself deep enough to write.

EDNA I think constantly that it's impossible but live through it. Half of the time I felt I ought to be buying bones and scraping the marrow out of bones, you know, and putting Gye on bread and really being a mother and the other half I want not to know that they're alive. And this is why women find it so hard to write because it's not their talent – they can suffer the talent – but being a writer is being a writer constantly, it isn't just when you're up-stairs or wherever one works, it is the most – it is the most exacting occupation. And at our peril, or at a woman's peril, she takes this on and that's why women's books and writing, modern women read as screams. Women like the Brontës didn't have children, or at least when Charlotte bore a child she died, George Eliot didn't have children, Virginia Woolf didn't have children, few women writers, Victorian, had children. And the ones who have now, like for instance the author of *The Pumpkin Eater*, find it a fierce battle. Finally the woman almost hates her children because they are the thing that tear her away from what she's committed to. I think women who write should not have children, because I think they do their children an injustice. I feel very guilty about –

NELL You do? You don't think this thing about having a mother who is developed and creative is possibly more of a good thing?

EDNA I think the experience of both conception and birth and being with the child is eminently valuable to the mother/writer but I don't know that the experience is valuable to the child. I think the child would like a happy mother, you know, and an extrovert mother, and to be a writer it's necessary to be a brooding person and to be an introvert. Obviously people survive it but I think there's a lot of damage done. Maybe when children are older there'll probably be then a sort of mental gel between the parent, the mother and the child but not when they're young – I know some children who told me the other day that they loved so-and-so and I asked the parent who so-and-so was and it's a woman, a dotty woman of about fifty who is always drunk and who when they go to the seaside, she lives somewhere down in Cornwall, she buries special little shells in the sand and she brings the children to look for the shells and accidentally they find these precious shells. They love this sort of woman. Now she is irresponsible in her own way, she drinks, and she is a bit dotty, but she has the kind of temperament that children would like, whereas I haven't, you know? I would want to write a story like that but I wouldn't want to go in the sand and bury the shells.

NELL I think children do like extrovert people, do like mums who are making cakes.

EDNA Yes, and curtains and all that.

NELL Who are sort of there when they want them.

EDNA And rightly so. The conflict is that if one is either schizophrenic or has a talent for two things it misleads them: by giving them the illusion of being a good mother and responsible and putting pearl barley in the soup, then suddenly you walk out on them, that's the damaging thing. This attitude of mine may be conditioning. Is guilt something we feel we should have or has it come to us from our own generation, from our own parents? Who knows? Maybe if one had a very good young girl in the house with children and one was working all the time they would not notice it. I don't know. I read something extraordinary the other day by Gerald Gardiner, who said he would change the abortion laws, or he would try to, and he said how absurd it should be that getting rid of six inches of flesh, of the body, is murder.

I thought as I read it this is marvellous because it comes from an intelligent man and from a man who it would never personally affect because he would never be pregnant so he's not saying it to save his own skin. And I thought if from the moment I was born I'd been indoctrinated in that way, about abortion, I might have, not a frivolous but a healthy and rational attitude to it, rather than having a deeply terrified Roman Catholic guilty attitude. Maybe it's the same about children. They say children in Israel who are in these public whatever they call them all day – crèches – are the happiest children in the world, and they only see their parents in the evenings. And there isn't this thing of two children, one wife and one sink all isolated away. It is our – we continue the crime if it is a crime – notion of feeling that we should do our duty.

NELL Yes but also that we get a tremendous amount out of this sort of intensely intimate sort of relationship with our children.

EDNA Well – I think the relationship or the intimacy of the relationship, strangely enough isn't always to do with being with them. Sometimes when I see my children with a lot of other children doing something particularly generous or particularly ungenerous, I feel very close to them and sort of know what they're doing. Or when I look in their pockets and find bits of cutlery and string and things like that, I often feel closer to them then than if they're sitting down driving me mad. But maybe that's selfishness on my part; I really want to indulge all the kind of memory and lyric part of them and not cut their toenails.

NELL Yes but I also have a great physical feeling. Yes, cutting toenails you see I like very much, I like bathing very much, I like holding my child naked on my knee and drying it and playing with it.

EDNA I think probably, when I hear you say that, that I'm obviously more neurotic about children than behoves a mother. When I first was handed my first, Carlo, I just cried in panic and you know how doll's arms come off and there's a wire through the body and the arm, I was certain that these arms were going to come off and when I looked at the top of his head where the split is, and that shiver the muscles do – you know, the shiver – I screamed because I thought the head was going to burst apart so you know, this is a terribly unnatural attitude to children and to birth even though I actually love the company of children, I love the honesty of children and their kind of open self-interest because that's the thing about them that's good. Somebody told me a story of having hurt his child's fingers in a motor car, and he said 'I hope you'll forgive me,' and I said that is the marvellous thing, children forgive everything, while they're still children. They don't realise that they have the right to penalise or to be vexed.

Later on of course they make up for that and really blame
and banish their parents, when they become adolescents
or in their twenties.

NELL But what does freedom mean to you?

EDNA Do you mean for a child or for myself?

NELL For yourself. What would having freedom
constitute?

EDNA Well I think I should take three things. Mental,
physical and emotional. Mentally I would like to be rid of
all the guilt and morbidity and notion of violence, hunger,
pain, all the things in the world that both are happening
to people at this very minute and that can happen to oneself. You know, when I see an ambulance going by with
a blue light, I panic. It never occurs to me that it might
be the ambulance driver going home to his tea. That's
one kind; the mental. That's why I think loss of memory
would be the only holiday in the world that I could ever
have because one's mind would be clear and empty like
clean blotting paper.

Emotional freedom: to be mature enough and generous
enough to love, either a man or a woman or child, particularly a man because it applies to men. To love them
without the need of weighing them down with it, without the need that they must love me, an eye for an eye, a
tooth for a tooth in return. I would love to love the way,
you know, it sounds a terrible word, but effortlessly, the
way the sun shines or roses bloom and to give the gift
of whatever I had in the way of conversation or love or
friendship to someone just totally and not ask. I'm not
sure that that's love, it's probably to do with religion. I
mean love in a practical sense, it mightn't work in life, it's
probably a notion really of loving God or Christ. Because I
find that on the whole when I have been in love or imagine myself to be in love, I become reduced as a person,

and my generosity, I mean mental generosity, is blighted because all the things come into it. I think 'Does he love me enough?' 'Will he love me tomorrow?' 'Will he love me the day after tomorrow?' 'Does he love his wife or his past love more?' Or whatever, you know. And that's very – well it's a reduction. And the third freedom I suppose is the physical freedom of, for one thing, of not being afraid of, say, blood, or cutting one's finger, or pain and also the freedom of – I have some sexual terrors which still maim me. I'm frightened of breastfeeding a baby, I'm frightened of having my nipples touched.

NELL Really?

EDNA Very frightened and I think of daggers and needles, and I think of – early on, from when I can't remember, the connection between sex and operations and medical things were all linked together. And I can't have the soles of my feet touched, I go mad. And this of course is very limiting because it stops one from having a completely relaxed physical or sexual relationship. In some ways I suppose it makes it more intense because one's capacity to release the self or enjoy the self is so restricted, then the time you do it's probably marvellous by comparison with the abiding tension. But I would like to have great physical freedom. It applies and sort of runs into all sorts of tributary things like not being able to ride a bicycle or dance or stroke a cat and they are all really connected. I long to swim . . .

NELL Would money, do you think a lot of money would make a difference?

EDNA No, not in the least. To have no money would be wretched. Apart from the fact that one would be hungry there would be the other things, for instance if I was sick or were having a baby, I would go out of my mind if I thought I had to have it in a house at home. I really would. So money makes a big difference technically, you know, just practical things; if I'm coming along the street late at night and I get very terrified by something, I am glad to have the money to take a taxi because it shields me from some painful and pointless experience. But having just enough money is as secure to me as having a lot of money because a lot of money would only mean that one had thicker carpets or two door knockers, or two doors, and that's nothing to do with living. The funny thing about money, I was thinking of it the other day in somebody's house and somebody said to me 'Now why do you young people write about sex now and don't write about money?' And long ago, he was talking about George Eliot, one knew when reading a novel what that person earned and you know, who brought the coal up. It was class and money but the thing about money now in our age is, it is only the rich who are really concerned about money now and who talk money. Where money around a dinner table becomes important is in a discussion about motor cars or winter holidays or some bloody feeble thing.

Among the poor if they're not that poor, or not hungry and among the middle and lower classes there's little talk of money. They scrape and they manage. It's only in the rich sets where it's all competitive and money sets has sort of – money is sex with the rich, they acquire motor cars that purr and ones that don't purr – I don't think it makes them free. It seems that the more money people have or when they really come into real money, it's then that the terror of losing it or risking wrong investments or being overcharged preoccupies them. It's an artificial terror, along with the ones one has from childhood! My God, an extra fear would be calamitous.

NELL I remember I used to be frightened of going at out without at least a pound in my pocket. You know, that sort of fear.

EDNA That's a good fear, because – no, it's the taxi fear. It comes back to the fear that you're going to be stranded or that someone's going to get a shotgun to you and you need to be able to make a hasty retreat. Really.

NELL But what sort of life did you dream of having when you were say 15 or 16?

EDNA Ah. Well this is a terrible thing – I don't mean a terrible question. It's frightening when I look back on it and try to figure it out. My dreams were so – what's like clouds – vaporous really, they were so inconcrete. For instance, a little bit away from the house there was what used to be called a chicken run. It was a wooden house that had gone very green, the wood had, from rain. And there used to be chickens there, and there was always the thing at night that one or other of us would have to go over and close the chickens up and put the stone to the door and sometimes one chicken, you know, you'd just be closing the door and one chicken would break out loose and then they all got out and the whole thing was anarchy. And I remember once saying to my mother (we had a workman who worked there with us and he was a marvellously kind, fat, real man who taught me how to read the time and how to ride a bicycle badly) and I remember saying to my mother once coming back from the chicken house, 'Will you give me the chicken house when I'm big?' And she said 'What do you want it for?' And I said 'I want to marry Torpey' (Torpey was his name) 'and we'll live in the chicken house' and that was obviously one very concrete dream of living with this genial man.

Alongside it – or not even alongside it but later, I had the notion of being with a very harsh, severe, granite-like man near a sea. A man who rode horses, in a sort of stone, gloomy castle of a house. And this man was both my liberator (he liberated me from a boring life and boiled eggs and closing the chickens) and he was able to make me a prisoner because I would not have any freedom. I would have to accede to him and I would be servile. I never had the dream of children, of having children, at all, which is very sick I think, unnatural. I also had the idea that my own family were very sad and irresponsible. My father, that is. My mother was a very sacrificial and wronged woman. And I thought that out in the world was the most beautiful, complete and adjusted people and that everything out there was marvellous. I mean I thought our house was awful, was gloomy, but it never occurred to me that the world itself was treacherous and that our house was just a little extension of millions of houses and millions of people. I never thought of going to other countries, I never thought of being, you know, anything. I just thought of writing stories and being in this stone jail with this man.

The thing about the men, the two kinds of men are sort of interesting in a way, about one's pattern in later life. I find that I am very fond always of jovial and genial men who would share a cigarette with you or if they were on an aeroplane would buy you duty-free perfume or, you know, a drink. I'm fond of them but I've never fallen in love with one, as yet. The odd time I've fallen in love it's always been with someone who is severe and who I know will become more severe. And this conflict really has done me a lot of – a lot of harm. It's a destructive way to love because one should like a man or the woman one loves whereas I feel I probably, deep down, fear them, and therefore hate them. Because fear and hate go together.

NELL But do you find the state known as being in love a satisfactory state to be in?

EDNA I long for it, the eleven and a half months that I'm not in it. I think there's a marvellous sensation – somebody asked me once when I was happiest – and I said, although I've since qualified that with another state of happiness, but anyhow I said then 'I'm happiest when I'm about to fall in love with a man who is about to fall in love with me.' And you know, that first hour, or day, or week, before the pain sets in, but then the doubt and the agony, this is what blights it. You see, I'd love to be in love and be able to go away to the North Pole or have him go to the North Pole and be totally enriched and nourished by the knowledge of his love, and be sure of it; be sure of his and of mine, or even be sure of mine because one should be content to love. Camus said, 'it is ill-luck not to be loved, but it is a tragedy not to love.' That is one of my precepts. I don't have it as yet, I'm anxious. I've had the physical lunacy, often.

NELL I think they're definitely two things. There is one which is that thing you were saying when the first kiss is really better than anything, it is really wonderful and with that first kiss one feels 'this is what life is all about, this is what I'm living for.' At the same time there is something else which is love which is the thing of time, you know, just being with someone, just being with them.

EDNA There's a beautiful poem of Yeats's which I think is the meaning of love:

A pity beyond all telling
is hid in the heart of love:
the folk who are buying and selling,
the clouds on their journey above,
the cold, wet winds ever blowing
And the shadowy hazel grove
where mouse-grey waters are flowing
threaten the head that I love.

And that marvellous solicitude, you know, that your loved one is in danger. I have this for my children. If it's raining and they're not with me I think 'they're out in the rain' and I suppose that's love. I haven't had it for a man much but I think I'm beginning to. I wrote a story once called 'A Woman at the Seaside' of a woman who had gone to the seaside to find a lover, not to find a lover in a sort of cheap way, but to re-meet a man who had been her lover when she was a young girl. They had romantic love, they kissed under trees. And she was since very unhappily married to a doctor who was an alcoholic and they used to have mashed potatoes on Monday, boiled potatoes on Tuesday, chips on Wednesday and really boring tedious living. And she manoeuvred it to go back to the seaside town with her husband where the lover was also. She manoeuvred it all, she met him, she and the lover managed to go for a walk, they walked along by the sea, and they went to a ruin and they were going to make love and he told her he was getting married shortly afterwards, and she said, 'Why didn't you tell me sooner before I lay down and sort of degraded myself?' He said 'I thought it would hurt you.' And she said 'Well, it's hurt me now' as she sort of gathered herself together and tidied herself up.

NELL But have you ever done things for the people you loved, like walked for miles through the rain to see them?

EDNA Oh yes, but I love doing that, but that's a different thing, that's indulgence.

NELL Is it?

EDNA Oh yes. Oh I think, you see, this is the great trap. I love it, and cooking things, you know more beautifully than they've ever been done, and peeling potatoes over-perfectly, but that's all — I don't think that's love. It's very pleasurable and one shouldn't I suppose stop doing it but love, I think love is sacrifice really and doing something that's difficult to do, that's the important thing. I haven't done that much.

NELL What does passion mean to you?

EDNA Unfortunately they're both totally allied. If a man I don't imagine myself to be in love with lays a finger on me I always freeze under his finger. Passion is so connected with love. And passion racks one's physical memory. Reliving it and re-dwelling on it. In bed at night, mostly at night. There's an electric lamp in my room that crackles every time a train goes by and I often waken thinking it's going to burst or something, and lying there I sometimes torment myself with reliving the odd hours – and they've only been hours, or at the most days – of passion in my life. So the passion is both the thing happening, the beautiful sort of sexual coming together and the reliving of it over and over again.

NELL And do you feel that this is possibly the best thing life has to offer?

EDNA I think not. I used to think it was and it was the thing in the world that I aimed for and I would meet some man – incidentally, just as an aside, I never feel passionate or desirous when I see simply a good-looking man or a titivating advertisement for underwear or something. It doesn't excite me the way brassieres are supposed to excite men. But to live for, I used to think it is worth the whole desert of you know, eleven months of the year, this month of absolute lunatic love, passion, breathlessness and not so long ago, or sometime ago, I had a relationship where I thought I was in love with someone who I thought was in love with me and when it sort of – it didn't end as much as it ceased to go on, which I suppose is a different thing – I think then it was that I really fell in love with the person. But I wasn't able or I didn't feel I was justified in telling him – in going ahead and sort of saying 'I now love you.' And I thought if I met the person again, or if we had tea, or slept together again, my having this love for him is of no consequence to him and I must contain it and not lumber him with it. Up to that minute in my life I had always thought that another person, mainly a man, would help me, in my needs. I always dreaded prison, or a hospital bed or a nun's cell or the places in the world where I would be alone with my own needs without the crutches of other people. And at that point, when I knew I loved this person who couldn't, for one reason or another, receive the love I had to give him, I decided or concluded I was in a cell and would be in a cell all my life and that everyone is in a cell consumed with need, or longing, or pain or one thing or another, and that the odd time they can come together is really very rare and it can't be sustained throughout a marriage – certainly it can't – at all, and then thinking of this cell I thought friendship, laughter, the sun, the sky, these are the things that endure.

I derive this from Camus's essays which I've been reading a lot and from the novel *The Outsider* where a man is waiting in the cell for the warders to come and bring him to be hanged, and according to Camus what will keep that doomed man sane and alive is the patch of sky that he sees through his window and the clouds going by. And as I get older I think that the price and premium I used to put on passion while loving a man or of being in a state of love, was really, not trivial, because I was very intense about it, but was superficial, compared with the enormous seriousness and loneliness of the whole of one's life. And what I think is most important now is that I shall resolve to manage, that each person shall manage, to survive everything, and look out the window at whatever is their bit of sky, and sink, not even sink into, but be glad of inanimate things, trees and sewerages, and advertisements, and cigarettes. Glad of the prevailing thing, rather than putting such hope into what is after all and must be by its nature, a very transitory thing, like fresh love.

This sounds in a way – you know, I can see people saying 'But what about your children, what about your mother and what about your father?' – I think you see that everyone is made up of so many different – what do you call the colours that there are in the rainbow – stripes, and that your children touch on one part – one territory of you, your friendships on another, your vices on another, but that there are sort of virgin soils there that nobody can reach, nobody can solve and you have to somehow address yourself, know yourself, change yourself and make yourself survive. I used to think the other things, that pity, and compassion were the most important things in the world, and kindness, and I still am all for pity and compassion and kindness, but I think survival is the most vital thing in the world and the strongest and finally the most honourable. Because if people hadn't survived the way they've done, and you know, when one sees a temple in Italy or the wall in Ireland made – a wall made at great jeopardy to the lives of men and women – one is enormously moved by that, by what people have done to make life liveable for you, for me. History gives us a sense of proportion. Our own little needs dwindle when we see what has gone before.

NELL Can we protect ourselves from being left by men?

EDNA Well, this is the big big fallacy. Far from protecting – this is indoctrination again – I think far from protecting ourselves we ought to learn to believe and know that this is going to happen. I don't mean that one should be bitter and say 'Oh, he's going to leave me in 1966' but this is what blights friendships and marriage and everything – is this little Cinderella dream that you get one man and one woman and that it lasts, you know, they live happily ever after. I think the marvellous thing would be for a woman, or a man – women fear it more, they fear being left more because they fear being stranded with babies – if a woman was able to say to myself and I've never met a woman who was (I wish we all were), 'It is beautiful for this moment and I'm with this man and the moon is round and tomorrow – God knows.' I think this would be splendid.

NELL Yes, this is one way but the other way is giving your whole self into making a life for that man. This is a way in which if you are left you are stranded because you haven't just given that moment.

EDNA Well of course, but – supposing you give part of your life into making a home for a man and then he hoofs off, at least it's been good and one has given – a woman, let's say a woman, has given because she wanted to and she got as much as she gave. We blame men and I do, and more men you know leave their shaving lotion in girls' bathrooms and disappear, than is justified. That is how they are. Whereas the fairly handsome, middle-aged man of 45 or 48 with a woman of 45 or 48, it is nearly always so, that the woman has spread a bit and the man is still quite attractive. This is biologically unfair and brutal. Fill in the scene by having a young girl go by in red jeans leaping up the steps and you know that that man wants to be with her and you know that he has every right to be. This is what's terrible. I find I identify with all three – I'm beginning to identify with the 48-year-old woman more – but what is terrible is that a woman has been brought up and is bred to believe that a man is hers for her whole life. It's unfair on the man as well as on the woman because either he has to get asthma or he has to be unfaithful or he has to do some mad thing to sink his own sadness, because a man must feel very sad when he can't impregnate every desirable woman in the world. A woman of 48 can feel awful, can feel bitter but if there was some tradition of her doing something else, digging up sea scrolls in Egypt or something, it would be marvellous and women would know that life had more than one goal. That is why careers are good for women.

NELL Yes, but I don't like the idea of doing something else because you can't have that, do you see what I mean, as the second best? That's what rather appals me about being 48, that's alright then, we'll have that, read or dig up scrolls but I don't want to do it just because I can't have men any more, because they don't want me.

EDNA Well, you see they want you in some area – they may not want to go to bed with you but they might want to give you a box of chocolates or ask you how they should deal with a young unfaithful wife. I mean it's all this thing that one must possess the man sexually and I'm sure if there was artificial sex – people keep telling me there will come a time when I can become pregnant at 80 – artificial insemination, sex through pinecones, the middle-aged woman would not be such a burden to the middle-aged man.

NELL This rather appals me. It's very obvious that thing about men not wanting one any more. It isn't exactly that I feel I shall be sexually frustrated or anything like that, I'm almost embarrassed at the fact that I should be sitting with a man who won't want to touch me.

EDNA Well yes, you'll feel degraded and humiliated, but isn't it equally embarrassing that he should have to touch you if he blooming well doesn't want to? It's a double trap.

NELL That's what I mean, that's what embarrasses me – that there'd be some knowledge between us that he doesn't want to touch me.

EDNA Yes, but who do you feel sorry for? Both. I'm

always attracted to men who are at least 45 and I know it is based on my fierce insecurity by a sort of quick unconscious mathematics. I think, 'Ah, when I'm 45 he'll be 70. He won't expose me to this thing that I dread' and I do dread it. What is terrible and in a way more hard for us is, with my mind I know what is intelligent and liberating and good and with my instincts and automatic behaviour I revert back to what my mother did and what my grandmother and everything, you know this thing of clinging on like a barnacle on a rock, to the man. There's nothing more distasteful than to desire a man who really finds you as attractive as an old grey candle.

NELL But you've chosen your men or have they chosen you?

EDNA I have a sort of neurotic tentativeness. When I'm attracted to someone I become ineffectual, I suppose it's an affectation. It would seem that they've chosen me. But I suppose I've chosen them in another way because I've given them signals that they can go ahead. I have a very incontinent heart really. I mean I fall in love and it drags me to hell and then purgatory, and then limbo, and I suffer, but I always know, no matter how in love I am, that I'm going to be in love again, with someone else, sometime in my life. I'm a bit ashamed of this and a bit dubious of ever becoming married again and ever entering into the situation that the stable part of me wants. You know, a man in bed at night, and cornflakes and all that. I think I despise it as well as wanting it.

NELL Do you find writing enough fulfilment?

EDNA I think I probably do. I sometimes look at my own life as if I was looking at a barograph (all those lovely inky waves on graph paper, they're done by a barograph aren't they, by a little wheel and a pen, a magical sort of pen which veers up and down), well when I look back on

73

the graph of my own life and the things I've done and the things I've sought out, it seems to me that I have always pursued pain and humiliation, and always emerged as a kind of auditor or surgeon in order to write about it. So I suppose it not only fulfils me, I suppose it is necessary to me and maybe more necessary than the relationships. This sounds terribly callous and maybe it is terribly callous, but I have gone into relationships, I mean intense relationships with men, obviously knowing that I was eventually going to write about them.

I'll tell you a sort of fantasy I had which bears out obviously this callousness in me. I was once very drawn to someone who was married and I once saw him wearing a dinner jacket, you know, long tails, long black tails and a white scarf and the white scarf had fringing and he looked to be another person in this attire. I hardly recognised him and then I had a fantasy that he came running towards me in exactly these clothes and that he was returning from the funeral of his wife and children and had in his buttonhole a black tulip and as he came towards me I took the black tulip out of his buttonhole and I put a white flower in his buttonhole. And we began to dance. Well now, this is a sort of very tiny but very, I think, revealing thing about how close to fantasy writing is. They're very close. To me the other life of the man I loved had no importance for me, not his wife, not his children, not even their funerals. And it's very − I suppose it's very callous, it's very inhuman although I don't care to think of myself as being inhuman.

NELL No, well what does it mean, 'inhuman', really?

EDNA Doing other people injury. I wouldn't do the injury in real life, but still my hope was of him widowed and I secure on this road/dancefloor.

NELL I think what you say about this thing of fantasy

means more than reality. It's fascinating really.

EDNA I suppose for some people fantasy takes over. I know from my childhood. A girl was having a baby once and she was not married and she knew she was having a baby because she went to the doctor, the local doctor, and he advised her to go to a seaside place and she sent him back a postcard and said 'I took the pills you gave me, and threw myself down the cliffs and nothing happened.' And then she came home. Her mother knew by then, because everyone read this postcard, the entire village, blind men read this postcard, and she came home from the seaside place and her mother said: 'Nobody is to speak to her until she goes to the doctor.' Nobody spoke to her, she came in, she was one of these very neurotic girls who sang, she sang silly popular songs like 'Cruising Down the River'. When she was unhappy she always sang 'Cruising Down . . .' And she went to the doctor again because he had sent a urine sample to Dublin to a hospital in order to confirm her being pregnant or not being pregnant. At the time I was full of sort of Convent shit, I said to her in a mean little voice, 'What's wrong with you?' both expecting and knowing her to say 'I'm five months pregnant' which was in fact the case. And she said to me: 'I've just been to see the doctor. He has just told me I'm sterile and that this will affect my whole life and I will never be on to marry any-body because I shall never be able to have children.' That girl needed help but she got none, not from me, not from anybody; I was such a little prig, and I regret it. What I find so alarming – is how she totally waltzed into fantasy, and just refused, really, to accept the brutal reality. Or, maybe it's a good thing. If the environment is awful, whether it's a concentration camp or frightening home or orphanage or whatever, if it's awful, the fantasy takes over. Strangely enough that girl lost her fantasy valve, she's a very practical girl now and she has 37 pairs of shoes, she buys shoe trees to put them in to keep their shape, and she would be embarrassed and offended if one referred back to that incident. It's not that she's grown up; it's that she's grown safe. I find my fantasies grow wilder with the years.

NELL This is very interesting because another thing which is very nice about you which is somehow connected − I can't quite see the connection − is how I always feel that if I was with you and I fell down or I got drunk or someone slapped me on the face, it wouldn't matter whereas with most people I'd be terribly embarrassed and I'd have to somehow keep my dignity.

EDNA Well, I think that is because I suppose one is only unashamed with people one knows are just as fallible or as foolish. Because the odds are that I would be falling down drunk at the same moment or if I weren't, I should be. Isn't it?

NELL Somehow I know that you'd be just as interested if I fell down drunk and got slapped in the face as if I was alright, or just somehow with me. I can't quite −

EDNA I know I would but − and this is a sort of continuation of what I was saying is reality for me. I went to somebody's house for dinner the other day and there were six or seven people there all talking rightly about where they'd been the night before and who said what, and you know, nonsense talk and there was one man who had a little cut, or rather a little bite, on his hand and the more I looked at it, the more I thought it was due to a tooth mark, and so I wondered if it was a lovebite and who had delivered it and when − the man's wife was jabbering away − I had an impulse to ask him who he'd last slept with. The trouble with these sort of questions are that people think you are being daring or being affected. In fact it is not the case, I would just as readily talk to a forester about how to sow young trees and how to protect them. What I am always trying to achieve is some direct and true flow of conversation between me and the other person and I find that where people are bunched together for a social evening, the conversation keeps sliding into inanities like who's fucking who or what shows we've seen and all that. It's why adjectives have become meaningless. The words 'marvellous' and 'super' suggest nothing because they're indiscriminately flung around. So that if you say there's understanding between us it is simply because we've met alone and often and always in an unceremonious way. If we met at parties we would probably be as empty for each other as most party attenders are.

There is somebody who helps me in the house who tells me the most extraordinary things, half-dream half-awake, of how her husband's penis has fallen off and they're in the bath and she's trying to stick it back on but her hands are slippery with bathwater and she's saying: 'For God's sake stand still till I get it back on.' And she tells me this naturally without any probing on my part. Once I met a woman in the laundrette and she said she was thinking of a summer's day when she went out walking with a man with a walking stick (she is quite old) and it was sunny and it was autumn, it must have been autumn because there were some ripe blackberries at the very top of a bush – the bush hadn't ripened all over – there were just a few black ones at the top and with the crook of his walking stick the man lowered the top of the bush and brought the berries within reach of her arm. She was thinking this while she was looking at her clothes going round in the washing machine. I think this sort of imaginative fantasy helps people to get through. Like Genet in prison writing *Our Lady of the Flowers*. The miracle of it: that this man was able to write this rich sexual book while he was doomed to masturbating and having bread and water. He, with that amount of imagination, would've gone mad if he couldn't write.

A woman told me a story once of having a lover – he was married and she was married – and once she had a fantasy she met the lover and he said 'I can't see you because my wife says she'll kill herself' and the woman said 'I'll go to your wife' and she went to the wife and said 'I'll scrub your house top to bottom if you let me see your husband every Saturday for half an hour' and in the fantasy the wife nodded and said 'yes' and out of nowhere there was a bucket and a scrubbing brush and soap and she knelt down and began to scrub a small linoleumed room and when she got to the last corner the wall just withdrew. She had to scrub a room twice the size and she got to the next corner and the wall again disappeared and finally she was scrubbing a mansion and she turned to say to the woman 'but I said your house' and the woman had gone. The door was locked. It had now become a big door with an old-fashioned lock on it and this was a frightening fantasy but still it was very liberating and helped her from her guilt. Worse than the fact that she was doomed to scrub for the rest of her life in this nightmare mansion, was the knowledge that he was waiting out in the street and he would never know why she hadn't come back.

Well, this kind of communication with people up to now has only been possible through writing and has only been possible through the very imaginative and the very fearless, because I think most people are ashamed of saying what's close to them. Most people would be ashamed to reveal that sort of dream or fantasy. Up to now it has only been in fiction and I think now it's possible, not in social groups, and not at dinner parties and certainly not at any other kind of party, but sometimes among people, especially women in fact, who are quite desultory and lonely, to have this kind of communication. I feel I know that scrubbing woman better or at least I know the side of her I want to know, better than if she, you know, gives a real inventory of the furniture in her house, or how much her husband's earned, or what side they made love on, whether backwards or frontwards.

NELL Yes, but also you're getting something special in people. Something original, beneath the sort of thing of how many sofas they've got.

EDNA Maybe it's escapism. I put too much value on what I call 'the octave range' in people.

NELL But how much do you make things happen to you or just let them happen?

EDNA I think I make them happen a bit more than I suppose I do. For instance if I overhear something in a bus – like one I heard the other day in a lavatory – I heard a woman saying to another woman: 'How is Arthur managing without his stomach?' and the other woman saying: 'Oh, very well as far as you can see.' She said 'You never know with that sort of thing but I say to him "Arthur read the paper and you'll know how well off you are."' And you think of the headings 'Nuns in takeover bid' and 'Child of nine raped'. So I then started chatting to that woman and I suppose I do make things happen but I'm getting cautious as I get older. The thing which a writer should never do is withdraw and I find I'm more inclined towards withdrawal now and being in the cave, than I used to be, and I read one of Kafka's diaries the other day which said 'I am so neurotic now I don't even hear noises any more' because obviously noises had been a big ordeal to him and he said 'it is so quiet, it's getting quieter and quieter, I'm sinking far away' and this thing, I think if one has been very wounded, and I have been very wounded,

there is the deep and sort of sensible instinct to get back
into the cave, and also to get back into the womb and one
of the things I'd love to do – as a sort of aside – to say
is the reason I think on the whole that women are more
discontent than men is not just that they get old sooner or
that they have the vote, or that they haven't the vote, or
that they bleed or that, but that there is, there must be, in
every man and every woman the desire, the deep primeval
desire to go back to the womb.

Now physically and technically really, as well as physically, a man partly and symbolically achieves this when
he goes into a woman. He goes in and becomes sunk-
en and lost in her. A woman never, ever, approaches that
kind of security. To some extent she's being violated or
invaded because when the maidenhead is first broken it is
a rupture. Each time and for evermore she must carry the
memory of that first rupture no matter how she desired it.
I'm sure the fear of pregnancy, whether people use contra-
ceptives or not, is still there too, because it's intrinsic, it's
an inherited feeling. There is a fear of pregnancy, there
is also the desire for pregnancy, the two things are battl-
ing in one. And the third cry to get back in the womb. A
woman never can. And that's why I think a woman can
never rely on a man the way she can on another woman or
the way a man can rely on the woman, because to a great
extent man is a woman's enemy. Even if in the centre of
her being she loves him, he is still her enemy much more
than she is his enemy because he can abandon her and get
on with his hunting but she cannot abandon him if she's
impregnated. Also the physical make-up of a woman is
so absurd. Technically it's haphazard. A woman can have
an orgasm from being touched by a man's tongue or his
hand or his heel just as much as if she is penetrated by his
penis. Therefore there is really no need, pleasure-wise, for

her to constantly run the risk of impregnation whereas a man's greatest and deepest satisfaction is not in suckling or arse-probing — homosexuals are always dissatisfied — a man's deepest need is to go into the woman's vagina, into the mother figure. What is so extraordinary about homosexuality is that a lot of the sexual aberration is the result of a mother-fixation and ironic that homosexuals should run from the very thing they most need which is the mother, and, going back in. They say the thing we fear rationally is often the thing we most desire.

NELL Do you have any definite moral code, do you think you know the difference between right and wrong? You see I think this is one of the problems almost of our generation, that everything seems to have gone from under our feet and why we're so insecure is that we —

EDNA — have no moral code.

NELL No moral code and we don't really know what we're meant to be doing.

EDNA I believe in only one or two sins, cruelty, killing, injustice. These are sins, everything else, lust, sex, adultery, covetousness are venial, you know, they're just little flaws. But I apply that moral code only to myself because I imagine I have intelligence and discipline enough to get through life sensibly. I ask different morality of my children. Once they went around the road singing carols at doorsteps under false pretences, they collected 28 shillings, and I said to them 'you're stealing, you can't do this, people are giving you money thinking they've given it towards a new bench in a church or something, when in fact you're going to buy lollipops with it' and I made them give it back. So that I have a moral code obviously, especially to people who are young and who are floating. When people are young they are floating and they don't know what is right and what is wrong, they don't above all else know the results or the consequences of the simplest action. This is my morality. I know now from experience that if I enter into something, or if I have a cup of tea with some woman's husband, that I must give regard to this in my conscience, and take full responsibility for it. The older you get the less need there is for society's morality, because you establish your own fierce rigorous morality, that your intelligence and your mind has hewn out for you.

As for us now, I think that oddly enough with the fierce sort of so-called freedom, sexual freedom, and Sunday orgies and smoking marijuana and all that, there is a much greater morality than there used to be. I really do think that. I think there's greater heartlessness and I think people at parties who say to each other, as I hear people saying at parties 'Feel like a fuck' is a terrible joyless thing really. But I think that in itself it reflects a sort of aching morality. Because they're not enjoying it, there's no abandon. It's summed up in that line in Harold Pinter's play which I think is so significant – the play was called *The Collection* and a man kept pestering another man and saying 'Did you sleep with my wife?' and is consumed with jealousy and the other man, who happens to be a homosexual and is living – or a heterosexual, who is living with a homosexual, says to the husband finally: 'No, we sat downstairs and we talked about what we would've done if we'd gone upstairs.' I think this is very typical of now. But even if they'd gone upstairs, what I mean is, even when the people who pick up a boy or a girl in the Tube and go home and make love even then there's nothing immoral in their action because the whole thing is nothing. It is as casual to them as going to Wandsworth Baths and having a swim. There's a fierce hollowness in relationships now. This creates a new morality. The morality of the lonely and the uncommitted. The uncertainty! The feeling that maybe it didn't happen — as in *Last Year at Marienbad*. I think morality is intrinsic to people's natures. It just takes on another complexion.

NELL I think the danger is that one treats different people by different standards. This is what I mean by we don't know what to do, because people act so differently but one tends to judge each person — the danger is saying 'Now what would she do to me?' I'm doing the same to her. This is all wrong but I definitely find this in myself.

EDNA How do you mean?

NELL Well I treat another person well because they treat me well, and I'll know another person will never — putting it on a very low basis — would never steal anything from me, so I'd never steal anything from them. What I mean is I know that someone would never look at my husband so I would never look at theirs.

EDNA I think I operate slightly differently, for instance stealing — I stole a scarf from a shop, about two years ago. It was the first time in my life I'd ever stolen anything. I didn't steal it, I picked up this brown georgette scarf and walked out the shop with it. And it was a time when I felt very very deprived, not just of goods, but contact, and it did give me a new — when I thought about it afterwards — a new insight into stealing, and people's need to steal. Anyhow I wouldn't give a damn if someone stole from me, it's not one of the things that worries me. If I were in love with someone I'd mind if they stole him but not goods. Morality is not the same thing as abstinence — I mean I say to my children: 'Of course sleep with people if you want to but don't beget children'. That's my morality. That they shall not bring into the world someone who isn't wanted, by them, and who certainly isn't at that moment going to benefit from being alive. But it's very important I suppose to evaluate what is good behaviour, as opposed to what seems good. I mean what are the good things one has done in one's life?

NELL What do you find erotic?

EDNA I don't know that I find anything erotic. Does that mean sort of sexually stimulating?

NELL Well, does the word mean anything to you? I think it means kind of visually exciting.

EDNA Then I don't really. I'm moved say, by snow or glass berries or the smell of mandarin oranges or dusk or things like that. Moved but not made erotic. No, I don't think I find anything erotic. What do you find?

NELL Strange things like – never things that have any connection with me at all – always things connected with other people, like girls' petticoats and things on other girls.

EDNA I didn't think erotic is the word. They sort of touch you and I find that too – I'm touched by the sight of a necklace on a bureau. But surely that's discovering some secret about the person.

NELL I'm touched by the sort of feeling of intimacy connected with the girl.

EDNA Isn't it strange that on the whole women are more touched by the external things of women like petticoats or dance shoes or something than by the external things of men?

NELL Yes, that's very true. There seems to be so much even in a woman's shoes, they're so much more telling than a man's.

EDNA They are, and the way the heels are and the inside whether the gold Paris lettering is intact. Does that make us a little lesbian? The word lesbian has such ugly associations, you think of sort of angular women with cigars and flat shoes. But there is in all women a love of girlhood, girlish things, and tulle and certain kinds of jewellery. These frivolous little possessions I love and am deeply moved and saddened by because I know that I reflect a state or a moment in a girl's life – like Camus talking of the young girls who come on the beach, he says they're like buds and next year other young girls who look identical come on the beach and are also like buds and no one knows where the girls from the previous year have gone to. And it's this fleetingness of girlhood that's one of the saddest things in life. It's sad for girls, it's sad for men. It's the peak of a girl's life, her budding, whereas it's not the peak of a man's life. A man is more beautiful and desirable probably as he approaches 30 whereas a girl is as she approaches 20.

NELL I don't entirely agree, I think women can become more beautiful and marvellous as they approach 30.

EDNA Ah they can become – I'm talking of the generalised feeling. A lot of women can and a lot of women are more beautiful at 30 then they were at 20 but the thing of girlhood is this young bloom and that early morning thing. Dew.

NELL But do you think one's capacity to love grows smaller as one grows older?

EDNA I don't. I definitely don't. I think in fact one is only capable of love when one is older. When one is younger, it's something else. You were asking me about what I live for? What matters? And this is the thing that matters, I live on expectation more than anything else. Of what I could become. I used to have hopes of what would happen to me, or that I'd go somewhere beautiful, or someone would touch my thighs or something, I used to have those hopes – I still have a bit – but I now have the hope of becoming a deeper person, of becoming a seasoned person. I may not. I have become self-obsessed, or I may die, or commit suicide, but the thing that I most live for is not only that I shall, but that the world shall and that we shall go out of life as remarkable human beings. Because we certainly don't come into life as remarkable human beings. Children are selfish little blackmailers. Adolescents are all very intense and bubbly but they're intense about themselves – pangs and private sufferings.

Each year and sometimes each month, I'm appalled by how little I knew the previous month. Not facts, although I wish I knew more facts, but I'm appalled by how insensitive I was, or how wooden I was, and the thing in life if there is anything in life, I suppose it is the development and self-perfection of human beings. Self-perfection in an outgoing way, I don't mean going into a monastery, or sleeping on a bed of nails, but the perfection which is able to help, be a positive help to other people. When you look at that table or that chair you see things that other people have made for you and somehow it's marvellous to realise that. I used to hope to be happy and I think that's an over-simplified hope because to be happy I suppose there are drugs in the world now that one could live on, and exist in a constant sort of euphoric blurred state of so-called happiness. But that's not living. It's too unintelligent. I don't know about religion or afterlife. On the whole I hope there is not an afterlife. If there is, and because of my wayward catholicity, then I am condemned to hell. And that's a sort of heavy load and an unnecessary load to carry around.

NELL I think the danger about this thing of getting older is that one gets harder. I think this is the danger. And things matter less. One gets hard because things have mattered so much one can't bear it, therefore one puts on some sort of cover.

EDNA I think that applies to destroyed peoples. I

sometimes see people who are obviously dead. They're walking around alive but they're dead. And ideally, suffering, no matter how great it is or has been ought to open people up to life but in reality certain blows kill people really, they get closed up. And this is tragedy. I don't think it's true of all people and it's not necessarily true as people get older; sometimes things, different things matter less or more. I remember when I was younger if I had done something slightly wrong to someone or failed in some petty little thing, I would have a fierce anxiety to go and make up with them. Now I would not have that because what matters to me, and this is the difference between young and old I think, what matters to me is not that I should run back and get into their good favour again but that I shall curb in myself the meanness that caused me to upset them. Well, maybe what I did when I was young was better, because I ran back and said 'It's alright, I didn't mean it' whereas now I wouldn't run back, I don't feel that's the important thing. So the values change. I don't think one necessarily gets harder, one gets probably more austere. And you expect austerity in others. I expect other people to be able to bear things as I feel I have borne things, and that's hard but it's also valid. The softness of youth is very nice and very necessary but it isn't very brave and certainly wouldn't make the world go round.

NELL Do you feel any particular fondness towards any part of your body like your hands or something?

EDNA When I look at other people I always look at eyes and the whites of eyes; I feel that intelligent and sensitive people always have beautiful eyes, it doesn't matter whether they're green or blue, or whether the pupils big or small, because their life shines through their eyes, and it quenches, and it comes on and it goes off. I have never sort of examined my body, my entire body. Even if I look at it I don't *examine* it because of my squeamishness. The words 'vagina' and 'womb', these words still fill me with terror. And if – not often – if it ever happens that a man admires one's body or the colour of one's nest of hair, I can't believe it, I'm always astonished.

So that on the whole the bulk of my body is closed to my enjoyment of it. So it's only the open parts like the face, the legs and the hands that I even can consider in this question. I dislike my hands because they're very child-ish hands but I get one great solace from them, which is, when I'm very tense or when I'm nervous, I clench my own hands and am somehow strengthened by it or I hold onto chairs, the sides of chairs, or else I grip stones or pebbles, or beads. Obviously I can sometimes stop my-self from falling over an emotional cliff with my hands by grasping something. But I don't think I have any pleasure in any part of my body, because my first and initial body thoughts were blackened by the fear of sin and therefore I think of my body as a sort of vehicle of sin, a sort of taber-nacle of sin. It is possible that this preoccupation with sin makes for a greater excitement in the act of love.

NELL How do you draw a balance between indulging oneself and refraining?

EDNA Well I think it's very easy. Everything one does, having a drink, kissing someone, buying a pot of jam, if it's something you want to do, then you're indulging yourself. If it's something you want to do and you don't do it, then you are refraining.

NELL Yes, but how often should one refrain?

EDNA Ah, well I think one should refrain all the time. Regrettably my life seems to remind me that I've indulged oftener than I've refrained. In theory I'm all for refraining.

NELL You are? I only refrain when I'm terribly hungry. I'll drink first because I'll be even hungrier and it'll taste better.

EDNA Then you're a complete indulger in that case. But I think indulgence is probably healthy if it's not doing anyone harm. However, I would like to restrict it in myself. I would like for instance to have the strength if on the point of entering somebody's house I saw the room beautifully lit up and the people beautifully prepared for conversation and lamplight and buffet tables, I would like to have the strength to turn round and go home again, cheerful, in other words to be able to contain my regret. Or if I loved someone to be able to approach his mouth and then draw back. However, as I say this, I recognise the fact that restraint can be another form of indulgence. I think balance is what counts. It would be marvellous to contemplate something like, say, a glass of milk for hours, to think about drinking it and how beautiful it was going to be and finally drinking it slowly and enjoying it. There is a tendency to confuse enjoyment with indulgence. As I say, I have always indulged but I'm not so sure that I've often enjoyed.

NELL What makes you go on living?

EDNA Well, it varies from day to day. Sometimes I'm just waiting for a telephone call or the next meal, or to pick my children up, but when I think about it and pose the question to myself I imagine that in time I would've become a different person and the world around me will be different too. There is this constant desire to break out of one's own skin and into another kind of reality. Sometimes you see paintings of rocks or ocean, or wilderness, and you think not only will I go there but I will partake of a whole new kind of experience. I will be born again through these rocks or in that ocean and the I who now suffers and laughs will do it in a different and possibly richer way. Talking of laughs I think of all the things in the world it is the one I put the most premium on. How many people have you met in your life that really make you laugh? Not enough. I used to hope, in a way I used to overhope and now it is not that I have lapsed into despair, it is that the business of hoping makes the present life null and promises false or over-glorified rewards. To go on living I would like to be able to get through all the minutes of all the days aware that they were the only ones I have and I had bloody well better make the most of them. I mean to go to other countries and do things, not in any missionary sense; there is no such thing really, because in doing good one derives good from it – but by being exposed to a totally new environment and set of values I imagine one is bound to be changed. I go on living in the hope that the I will either become lost or changed, possibly what I'm fumbling towards is some kind of God but I would like him – there are no She-Gods – to be on earth rather than in heaven.

EMMA

Twenty-nine; has a daughter and a son

EMMA Duty probably does pay off in the end, doesn't it?

NELL Yes, that's the awful thing.

EMMA I don't think there's any way round it.

NELL And I think the only way to keep a man is by being really nice, making a nice home.

EMMA And you should actually knit. How can a man be unfaithful in *your* hand-knitted jumper?

NELL I feel very much this about my children, I feel they're tremendous protection against any other women.

EMMA They should be, but they're not always, are they? They can be used as a lever against you just as easily. And also you know I'm always packing up to go or rather looking at my wardrobe and not finding anything to pack, and you know, I just couldn't leave those kids. I think Peter's got the upper hand on it because he could.

NELL Is he not so much involved because he's a man?

EMMA They think they're not. Possibly they change their minds – a week later, but a week later some other thing may have happened.

NELL Well, what Jeremy said he felt most when he wasn't here was he couldn't bear the thing of waking up in the morning to an empty house.

EMMA Yes, but if you went off with somebody, which is usually the case, you wouldn't notice would you? You'd be having a lovely time with them all the time. And there wouldn't be those beastly kids coming in to wake you at 7 o'clock in the morning saying they wet their bed or something.

NELL But why do you think you got married in the first place?

EMMA Oh, just to please my mother. I felt terribly guilty just to go home at the weekend in our little Austin Seven, have food and wash up and off we'd go.

NELL And did she use to say, 'When are you getting married Emma?' and all that?

EMMA No, no, she never mentioned it, I just felt terribly guilty – terribly middle-class.

NELL Why middle-class?

EMMA I am, you know, in my thoughts and everything. Peter and I had been going around for six years before we got married. How people can meet and get married in a month or two months – they must have fantastic faith and optimism.

NELL But didn't you begin to want children?

EMMA No, I never wanted children.

NELL Why did you have Anna?

EMMA I didn't really want either of them. I was horrified.

NELL I thought you always wanted a little girl.

EMMA When I was going to have one I wanted it to be a girl, yes, but I didn't really want one at all.

NELL Then what would your life consist of if you hadn't had them?

EMMA I don't know. What it's going back to now, I suppose. Socialising, just nothing you know.

NELL But would you like to have a big sunny flat in Chelsea and lots of time and lots of boyfriends, and enough money to live on?

EMMA Yes I'd love that.

NELL Can you imagine being without your kids, you're very much part of them aren't you?

EMMA Yes. I'm terribly passive.

NELL But you wouldn't accept the fact that somebody came along to you and took you away from them – you wouldn't let it happen?

EMMA No, I wouldn't let it happen. This is the middle-class bit that you have animal instincts of preservation. It's all laid out for preservation isn't it? And if you conform to it naturally without living in the suburbs, actually you know inside you that this is how you feel –

NELL I could never understand how easily my parents and my parents' friends got divorced, because the idea of divorce really horrifies me, it sickens me with terror.

EMMA Yes, me too.

NELL And I really sort of feel that one's only got one chance to make a decent life and after that one would feel too submerged by nostalgia.

EMMA Yes. I couldn't do it, I couldn't start with some-body else. I think one should let each other have complete freedom because in the end (I know it sounds ideological) but in the end if you do come back and want to come back it's the right thing, you know. Why should two people because they're married cut themselves off entirely from other relationships? I'm sure that what they suffer from making mistakes helps doesn't it? It must do.

NELL Yes, I think it does, but I think it's this great thing of risk. I'm still amazed at how we are together after all this. God knows, we could be apart but somehow everything has come alright in the end and we're very alright at the moment.

EMMA Perhaps it was your sheer tenacity, tenacity of

wanting to stay together, which honestly is a marvellous gift to anybody, the fact that somebody wants them. It's giving more than love.

NELL Well, it's very difficult because there's this line between. Sometimes men want you to be all over them, boosting them up, waiting on them hand and foot and then suddenly they don't want anything to do with you, they want to be all aloof and distant. That's what's so impossible about relationships, people change what they want.

EMMA This is it. Peter has gone through all this too.

NELL But there seems to be no rules, what I mean is you can't set yourself any sort of rules really because people want different things all the time, that's what I find so agonising. But do you think it's worse for our generation? Are we sort of more difficult to please?

EMMA I should have thought that somebody in your position probably was. Not so much in Peter's and mine.

NELL Why not so much with Peter and yours, because you've got less financial freedom you mean?

EMMA Yes, could be and also I think there is this middle-class bit again. I don't know – all my friends split up I suppose. I just think we're immune from it quite honestly, if I look into what I really mean, I just think that Peter and I are just different, that we would never part, you know, that we just need each other terribly. I can't often think beyond that.

NELL I feel that too, but I also feel there is no other man I've ever come across that I could live with. I can imagine a man I could find terribly attractive, all that kind of thing, but I can't really go further than that I can't imagine not resenting terribly having to cook for them and wake up with them.

I'm suddenly full of resentment at the idea.

EMMA Yes. For years I used to look for somebody when I got used to having Peter around but I'd always in the end come rushing out and say 'I must go now' and go off to Peter. Suddenly they would repulse me, just by looking at them or something they were doing that I just couldn't bear any more.

NELL But the other thing I do think is funny about 'our lot' is that we've got no moral code, we've got no way of knowing what's right and what's wrong.

EMMA No, this is the terribly confusing thing because I do think that you should have complete sexual freedom, but then I think of course if you do you're forfeiting something because the code isn't thoroughly accepted all round. It's sort of half-accepted in theory but not in practice. If I was to go and sleep with the only person I should like to, Peter would never forgive me. But he says to me, 'Yes, go and sleep with him. Yes, go on, do you good,' all this bit, but I know in his heart he hasn't got that far, and I think that is difficult because you do hear of people sleeping together all the time and perhaps they can be sorted out, but in this duty to wife and family thing I know that I'd jeopardise something quite seriously.

NELL Definitely you would. You're in a terribly strong position never having been unfaithful to him.

EMMA Terribly strong. But is it worth it?

NELL I think it is really. If you're alright I think it is. I mean sex is so little in a way, it's so little to go off with somebody else. What is it? Waiting on a draughty street corner for an hour.

EMMA I don't know how people do it.

NELL But the other thing is I always think any girl who goes out with Jeremy I think, you know, 'the bitch, what's she doing going out with him?' That's my reaction. Yet if I was asked out by a married man, if I wanted to go I go, I wouldn't think about the wife. What do you think about this?

EMMA The same until it comes to the point, and then I get guilty.

NELL I don't, that's the funny thing, I don't get guilty.

EMMA I don't know, I've had so little experience. But the only occasion when I could have precipitated something, I didn't want anybody to see, I wanted to get out of the thing as quickly as possible. If I could've been absolutely sure of not being found out I would've gone ahead.

NELL Of course that's a great thing, not being found out.

EMMA As it was, it wasn't any good and I would've been found out. It all loomed much too big.

NELL You act instinctively, you don't not do this because it's adultery or you don't do this because it's cruel.

EMMA No, it's all in me, I've got it all there, I don't have to even think about it. When I'm drunk I try not to be drunk, when I'm going to faint I stop myself, when I'm going to be sick I stop myself. I'm a Quaker. My father was a Quaker and I'm sure that I've got it all in me, I'm a dreadful prude. Jimmy, a friend of ours, is always trying to get me drunk at parties, Peter's in Manchester or somewhere and I'm absolutely reeling and I appear to be beyond anything but I never let go. Just never.

NELL Well of course that is a great thing if you're able to let go. I can't do it. It's just beyond me. I could never not come home to my own bed at night.

EMMA No, I couldn't either. I could never break that sort of cord you know. But I always put it down as prudery, I don't know what it is. Morality.

NELL I don't know either. I just can't let things go.

EMMA It's terrible, this is what I always put down to the middle-class bit again. I don't know what it is, I can see it in my father he goes even farther than I do. He pays bills before they're asked for and things.

NELL Can you imagine living in a world where there's lots of different boys coming and going?

EMMA I couldn't cope actually. This is what I would love to do. I could've done it but I just couldn't cope. I'd love to just take off to somewhere like Tangier or something and just never come back, it would be absolutely marvellous but all I do is to go to the Inner Circle and come back.

NELL Do you ever have a great nostalgia for your past?

EMMA No, because I feel better now than I have ever felt really.

NELL Why is it that you feel better now?

EMMA Well, somehow men seem to accept you more with kids and husbands and things. I always used to have dreadful battles with people expecting one to sleep with them.

NELL And now they don't say much?

EMMA No. I've got it very well organised now but I don't know how long it'll last.

NELL Everything changes all the time doesn't it? But I feel much better than I've ever felt because I feel in a position of power to choose. One isn't kind of fumbling in the dark through a sort of forest of agony and pleasure. One definitely knows what one's doing.

EMMA Definitely. I think it's the ideal age actually. Providing one can keep one's looks sufficiently, you know.

NELL But how long can one keep one's looks?

EMMA Another five years I suppose.

NELL You think that's all? And then what happens?

EMMA I suppose that's when you reap the reward of being faithful and dutiful. And you turn to something else which fills the gap then. Like embroidery. And quite like it, you know. Bridge parties even.

NELL But our friends go on getting older with us.

EMMA And they'll look just as attractive I suppose — I mean now I look at people younger, Fulham's full of these delicious boys who are all long-haired and lovely — just how I've always wished boys should be — and you look at them, because I stare at them quite blatantly — and they've got completely empty faces, it took me ages to realise what it was — that I used to be disappointed when I looked into their faces. I realise they just hadn't got those little subtle lines — they're just lines, which makes faces more interesting. I need to see faces like this.

NELL And one needs to be with people who've been through it in a way, who've been through it and have suffered and who know what it's all about.

EMMA I get so intolerant of crassness. I should loathe to be 17 again. But I'd like to stay at this age for a good ten years. Really, I think it's a marvellous age.

NELL I don't mind at all being sort of 35 or 40 but I — I think when one starts getting to the end of the forties and starts having aches and pains, feeling tired — that's much worse. But I think I'd like to have a couple more children when I'm about 38.

EMMA Yes, that might be an awfully good idea.

NELL Then that will keep you going for a bit you see.

EMMA I always did feel when I was having them that I was missing out on things, because I left it long enough anyway.

NELL You felt by having them you were wasting a year? I never felt that because I rather like being pregnant, in that it gives me an excuse to kind of get out of it all. It is the final — when everything's getting too much for me I get pregnant, you get out of it, nobody can attack you.

EMMA I don't know. Actually Peter attacked me more

when I was pregnant which was rather nasty but he really made me terribly miserable. Peter must have somebody who can fight him back the whole time and you can't when you're pregnant. I couldn't. I just collapsed and he didn't care, he didn't realise. He'd just go out, you know.

NELL I could never take criticism from anybody except when it's given with complete love. I can't bear people criticising me, fighting me, saying nasty things to me.

EMMA No, oh gosh no. If anyone says something nasty in a conversation I don't listen to anything else for the rest of the afternoon, I'm thinking about what they said.

NELL But what sort of life did you imagine that you would have when you were sort of 16, 17, did you think of a life you'd like?

EMMA No, I didn't. This is the cowlike, passive thing, in me. I never thought about it and just expected it to happen – I'm a terrible 'live for the moment' person.

NELL How much of your time do you live in the future?

EMMA None of it at all except the occasional horror thought about looking old.

NELL Of course it's the most difficult thing to live in the present.

EMMA No, it's easiest.

NELL I don't think so, I think living in the present is the great secret of happiness. By living in the present I mean enjoying the things you've got to do as well. Quite enjoying ironing, or is that different?

EMMA No, I resent any form of work. I'm terribly lazy. I hate it.

NELL Everything seems to be done when anyone comes to your house, there's always tea. There's no feeling of cracking, you know.

EMMA Well, I live for the present so much that I had to do the dishes before I left even though I knew I was terribly late because I couldn't think beyond doing the dishes. You know, it's complete lack of willpower.

NELL Do you sort of resent the thing of cleaning rooms, do you feel it's an awful waste of your time?

EMMA Dreadful, yes. My mother spends her whole life keeping her house immaculate and you know, it'll be there hundreds of years after she will.

NELL Is it because one can't bear it dirty?

EMMA Yes it must be I think. I suppose it's much easier and much pleasanter to live in something clean isn't it?

NELL Would having a lot of money radically change your life?

EMMA I think so but it probably wouldn't, would it?

NELL How would you change it?

EMMA Well, half of our life's worry is money. Christ, we owe so much money everywhere, we owe thousands, it's terribly depressing. We can't afford to pay it back. It gets more every week.

NELL What else would you do when you paid the money back, would you like someone to look after your children?

EMMA I wouldn't want them to do everything. Like this evening we were going to the pictures, Peter said 'let's go to the first house' and I said 'we can't because I've got to put the kids to bed.' Lyn could put the kids to bed but I just close up because I know that I want to put them to bed. I've gone off possessions – no that's not true – I've gone off nice things.

NELL Have you?

EMMA It's so easy to buy things now – like in the way of clothes. When I first started being interested in clothes you couldn't buy nice things and you had to make them. Now Mary Quant and all the others do really super things I'm not at all interested in them any more.

NELL Is this true of objects?

EMMA With houses and furniture – with all the things I've always liked and collected, anybody can go and buy now – they've become fashionable.

NELL After you'd had Anna and Frankie did you feel very different?

EMMA I was terribly depressed for ages. When I found I was having Frankie I nearly went mad. But I never feel different. That's a terrible thing about living for the moment because – I can't remember what I felt like before. So I never feel different.

NELL Yes. But you have a very good memory, you can often remember what people have said, little things.

EMMA I've got a photographic memory for situations. I can remember the whole scene, it's like a great film. I'm not in it, I'm just the camera.

NELL Do you think back on times?

EMMA Yes I do, I think about them quite a lot, but there's such a lot I can't remember, this is what frightens me. Years and years I just can't remember.

NELL Do you think that knowing people a long time makes you much fonder of them?

EMMA Yes, that's why I get terribly upset when somebody like Felicity can just cut me dead when I feel that I've got a complete bond with her.

NELL A complete ally, somebody on your side?

EMMA She's sort of almost a blood relation. I could never, ever, cut anybody dead when I've known them so well. I couldn't do it. Even if I was hating them at that moment I'd have to say hello first.

NELL Do you feel that one of the great problems is communication? Even between husbands and wives, that it's so hard to say 'You're hurting me,' or 'Tell me about it,' or 'Comfort me?'

EMMA It is hard isn't it? God went wrong.

NELL What is it? I sometimes feel it's because we're frightened that people — that everybody else is alright and we don't want to show we're not alright?

EMMA I always think that the other person does know and I think that words — apart from not being able to say the words — I think that you shouldn't need to, because they should understand, you feel that they should know instinctively what you're thinking about. And often I've looked at Peter when we've been having a row and he's been saying this, that and the other and I've thought it all and I've just looked at him and it's all there, you know, I know all the answers, all the reactions and everything but I think if you don't understand there's no point anyway in saying them. And you just don't seem to have the energy, I don't know why.

NELL And also one can remember, you know, when one does feel particularly sort of — saying 'Well,' (towards the other person) 'you are my life and I really do love you' and sometimes I want to say 'I love you and you mean everything to me', but one can't even say that, can't even say the nice thing to someone.

EMMA We do sometimes manage to do that but that's the only thing that keeps me going, the fact that Peter just does occasionally, after being absolutely foul for months and months, says 'I need you and I couldn't live without you'.

NELL But it's hard to say it then and it's hard to say when they're being nasty to you. It's very important to say it, it's marvellous that Peter can say it. But how important do you think sex is?

EMMA Oh well I'm sexless I'm afraid. That's one of the big problems. I just wouldn't care if I never had it again really. It's terribly sad.

NELL Do you think it is sad? I think possibly it's rather

a good thing.

EMMA I think it's sad really.

NELL Sex really is an awful lot of trouble and an awful lot of pain.

EMMA It's rather awful not wanting it ever because that causes pain. Because obviously it makes Peter think I don't love him and it makes him feel that he's being foolish.

NELL Yes, that is true too. But you don't get that terrible thing of resenting someone for not making love to you. You don't – I think one of the most awful things that make women terribly bitter is that they really hate men or a man or their husband for not making love to them enough.

EMMA No, I don't get that, in fact I'm always very relieved. This is why it's so easy for me to be faithful.

NELL That is true, because you can go ahead with your emotional involvements in your own quiet way.

EMMA And it doesn't involve me in it.

NELL It's so interesting really because you do see beauty and all that means a lot to you and it seems to me that in a way one's response to beauty is quite a sort of sexual thing.

EMMA I think it's a sex substitute.

NELL I have absolutely no suicidal urges at all. I've been terribly depressed, sort of agonisingly unhappy at times, but it's just never occurred to me.

EMMA I've thought about it but know that I would never do it.

NELL I haven't even thought about it when I've been terribly depressed.

EMMA Not even out of sort of martyrdom?

NELL No, I couldn't bear to hurt people that much by killing myself. I couldn't bear to hurt Roc that way.

EMMA Actually, you're quite right, I haven't thought about it since I had the kids. I did once walk to the river.

We only lived around the corner . . .

NELL Do you think women are any different from men in any particular way?

EMMA I think they're entirely different. I don't understand men at all. I don't really like men actually.

NELL I think women are much more fascinating.

EMMA If a man comes into the room – even if I'm not interested in them I still can't help but try to make them approve of me. And often to the extent that I cease to talk to the other woman but given the choice I could always talk to the woman. I prefer to be with them.

NELL I care more that women think a lot of me than men.

EMMA Yes, I do too. In fact I don't really care what men think about me at all. But in fact even if I think they are unattractive I often say things which I know it would suit them to hear. But really that's a form of looking down on them because I wouldn't do this with a woman. It's really just appeasing them, to keep them in their place or something. You can't be bothered really. Putting some sort of wall between us? Glossing over, sort of pot of varnish.

NELL Do you think life is really a tragic thing?

EMMA Yes, I do. It shouldn't be but it is. We seem just to be here to be paying debts somehow. Possibly it's because we're so dreary about money at the moment you know. I didn't always think it was tragic. This thing that people can be of my mother's age and have no friends and be nice people, really nice people, you know, my parents are really straightforward and honest and nice people and yet they don't seem to have any friends. And this inability to communicate about things you really care about, I think human beings are totally unequipped. Why should it be miserable, why shouldn't everything be lovely? It could be lovely couldn't it?

NELL Yes. So many lovely things and things to do. Possibly one is terribly bad at organising one's life you know, when I think of all the sort of lovely things like going swimming and one just never does them.

EMMA Because there are so many trivial, irritating, stupid things stopping you. I think it's all a tragedy actually. The fact of getting old is a tragedy really. And just you know, this total inability to communicate to more than one's children really. Anna at the moment is fantastic because without speaking or doing anything she will go upstairs and get something which I have been thinking about. Yet I don't often understand her. She's so like Peter and I don't really understand him. Frankie I can understand better because he's more like me.

NELL And do you get on quite well with Frankie now?

EMMA I never will I don't think, he's too like me. I'm not interested in him enough to bother, because I think I can understand him. This is a thing about men, the only men I really like are the ones who are unpredictable really, I don't know what they're going to do. Either I don't want to know them because of this or I'm fascinated because of this, the two things, you know.

NELL What will you try to teach Anna about men?

EMMA I'm afraid I've fallen into the great thing of saying to her I don't like them which is rather dangerous.

NELL Have you told her that already?

EMMA I think I have, yes. It's very difficult not to, I mean when I'm in a really bad mood I let all sorts of snidey things slip into the things I'm saying. I think one has to when Peter behaves so irrationally, you know, in front of them.

NELL So what do you say to them?

EMMA Afterwards I say, 'Oh well he's bad-tempered, he can't help it,' which is about the only thing you can do.

NELL Does it worry them when he does that?

EMMA Oh then they say, 'Oh daddy was naughty.' 'Why is daddy naughty?' I say 'Oh well, he can't help it, he's bad-tempered.'

NELL Which is the truth of course, isn't it? It is the truth.

EMMA I don't think there is any point in glossing it over really. I don't know what I shall teach her. She's terribly sexy anyway.

NELL So it wouldn't harm her to be told you didn't like them?

EMMA Not really no, because I think she likes them. You see, I've got this great theory anyway that people are exactly what they are when they're born and nothing really that you can do is going to change them that much. You can protect them by being perfect and doing everything you should do to help them and cherish them along but eventually they're going to come bump and it's all going to happen in a year instead of having it happen over a period of time, they've gradually been broken in, I mean life is horrible, isn't it? People are cruel and beastly and people don't care how you feel or react and things and I think you might as well have it a bit rough when you're little to get you used to it. And I think this 'Listen with Mother' and things isn't really fair because life just isn't like this.

NELL Well I always think this about the advertisements on television with the lovely clean home and the woman in the apron doing her hands. But I find this is so filling oneself with lies, this thing of the television advertisement, I think it could make somebody who is less strong or less in a position to get out than I am, feel terribly inferior. Because you get the idea that everybody's house is like that, neat and clean, and you know, you feel –

EMMA I think there's going to be the most dreadful

dreadful wave of nervous breakdowns and suicides in the next 10 years, because look at these kids growing up – they expect everything. Their mothers have bought them clothes. When I was a girl, you know, we had parcels sent out from America and I never had new clothes. When I went to art school my mother bought me two dresses and a coat and I can remember them now, these two beautiful dresses I'd had bought and ironed them and washed them – you and I was 17, 18. Whereas Lyn, typical, and Brenda, they're going to expect the earth aren't they and they're just not going to be able to afford it. I mean if Peter and I run into fantastic debt and we're really very careful and sensible with it and I really do think that we have been as economical and thrifty as we could possibly have been, they're not going to know what happened. They're going to feel so mixed up – the perpetual television advertisements of these fabulous places, all the gadgets, all the gear, you know – everybody seems to have everything and everybody will have everything, tape-recorders, gramophones, but really, normal people can't afford it all. I think this may have happened in Sweden. They've got the most fantastic suicide rates haven't they? And they say it's sexual freedom, or the Northern Lights or something but it's probably pure keeping up with the Joneses.

NELL Do you feel like you've made any big mistakes in your life, that you'd like not to have done certain things?

EMMA No, I'm quite smug about my life really. I think really I've done the best I could have. I do wish that I hadn't been such a pioneer, I wish I'd been a little later. Either a little earlier or a little later, I think we came at a bad time. When we walked around when I was a student we were stared at in the street and pointed at as freaks. Nobody looked like us. In 1951 I looked like this, I really didn't look any different. Nobody looked like us. My mother was a social outcast because of me in the street. People laughed at our clothes and laughed at our make-up and our hair and jeered and shouted at us down the street. Kids have it so easy now but that in itself had certain rewards because you felt you were something and somebody looked at you and you were just one of the mob but then people exploited this. Look it's like you know us saying about not wanting the clothes, not wanting the furniture so we lose out all round in actual fact you know.

NELL But you've never been ambitious really have you?

EMMA No. I wouldn't know what to be ambitious for. I could never decide what I wanted. I always wanted to be famous. Well I've spent all my life in sort of theatrical, well till I was 12 I went to a dancing school.

NELL And you never tried to become famous by becoming an actress or something?

EMMA No, I haven't got enough talent. I knew I hadn't.

NELL But do you feel you've got confidence now you've got the confidence of knowing you're alright and everything?

EMMA Yes I do actually. Although I look incredibly shabby when I go down Regent Street!

NELL But that's another thing you know.

EMMA It would be lovely, having worked so hard and having pioneered this look – one only goes to the cinema now – we went to see *Goldfinger* in Hammersmith the other day and everybody in the queue one could have known, the way they dressed and the way they looked their expression – ten years ago there would have been one other person in the queue perhaps and you would have known them. And I like seeing everybody looking how I like them to look, you know I think this is the right way to look but I feel terribly lost and I want to shout 'I started all this, we started all this.' Though people would just laugh at you.

NELL What do you get most out of doing now?
EMMA I don't know actually. Talking I suppose.

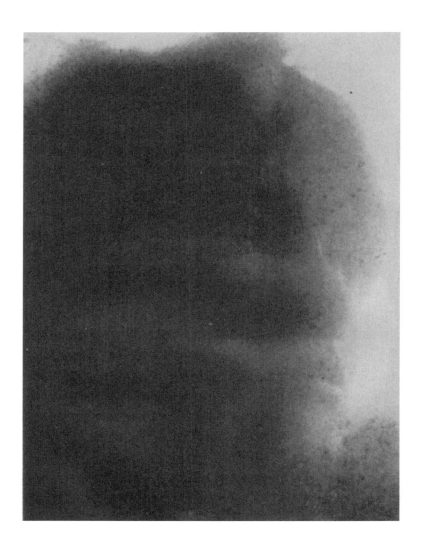

ANTONIA

Twenty-six

NELL Have you got any idea of what sort of a life you'd like to lead?

ANTONIA Well, I think I want — to have a bit of everything. I don't want to lead any set sort of life. I want to have children terribly and I feel that I should've had them a long time ago. I've missed something so much. I wanted one about six or seven years ago, I wanted one as soon as I lived with Ben. And it was impossible because of the house and this and that. And actually we put it off and put it off for reasons that were quite irrelevant — we ought to have had one a long time ago because it would I think have held us together much more. We've drifted so much now and now that I'm having one there's nothing, no sort of harmony. I remember I thought I was pregnant about a year after having lived with Ben and I told him about it and at first we were absolutely terrified because it all seemed so complicated and then the tremendous closeness that it brought because I thought I was, was so overwhelming, so marvellous and we haven't had that this time at all. If anything it's put a tremendous barrier between us, and it's a sort of fight really.

NELL Why, does he feel slightly you tricked him into it,

you mean?

ANTONIA Well yes, partly, because I did, I just thought I'd go on forever not having them unless I did, because Ben would never say.

NELL But yet before, earlier you felt you shouldn't trick him into it? Why didn't you have one the first year?

ANTONIA I thought his reasons were quite reasonable but actually they weren't, in a way. The only reason that was reasonable was that the house was unsuitable to have children in, but you know, under pressure you get things done. I always used to put Ben's things first you know. I always used to follow Ben which I don't now so much, I follow myself. Anyway, it's sort of important to have children to me and I want something else like painting. I enjoy doing it, to keep a balance and also to keep myself separate and have something always to fall back on I suppose if I'm not happy. I always feel I've got something although I don't do it very much. I don't work hard or anything like that. I like to have it because it's just something that one can fall back on.

NELL Do you think this need to have children is an instinctive need?

ANTONIA I think it is with some people, I think it is with you, isn't it? I've always got that impression but there aren't many people who I feel it is like that.

NELL I definitely feel it's a sort of opting-out for a time, if one's pregnant, no one can get at one in any way.

ANTONIA Well I suppose I thought this in a way. It would seem that anyway. Because I did it at a time when everybody – Ben particularly – seemed to be getting at me but he got at me much more I think because I was pregnant because he resented me for being pregnant. In fact I've never been so miserable in my life as I have been since I've been pregnant. I've never been so unhappy, ever. I think with Ben it's because he's just overwhelmed with responsibilities or he inflicts responsibilities on himself and things get him down terribly, and he just doesn't want any more. He didn't want the dog, you know, but he loves it now.

NELL But do you feel that you can start all over again with someone else?

ANTONIA I was thinking about this. Yes, well, I do sometimes, you know – especially when he's horrible to me, I think I could easily because I get terribly involved with other people and I think it would be so marvellous and I've even got so far as looking for a house and doing something really constructive about living with somebody else.

NELL So that you found a nice place –

ANTONIA Yes. Then – I love all my things so much, I couldn't leave them and I couldn't take them because they belong to both of us and sometimes that's the only reason that stops me. I suppose it's much deeper than that really. I get terribly attached to people I'm with and I often have felt I could never love anybody like I've loved Ben. I don't think you have the capacity to love more than one person like that, apart from anything else, if you get hurt you sort of don't believe in that sort of love any more. If it fizzles out as it has with Ben and I, it's changed so much, I feel now a sort of tenderness to him and I'm very fond of him but there's no big passion or anything what there used to be.

NELL No but you still care about him don't you?

ANTONIA I care terribly about him.

NELL So if you found a nice place –

ANTONIA Well ultimately but I care about him more when I'm not with him than I do when I'm with him. I resent him terribly when I'm with him. Because I'm unhappy with him I suppose.

NELL Say when you're lying in bed at night with him, then do you sort of feel this is the person I love, this is my life?

ANTONIA Well no, I find myself thinking would I really be happy if I left him? Why do I go on with him because I'm not happy with him at all. And why do I go on spinning it out? I'm in a terrible dilemma I find because it's not so much what I feel for him now as the past. That one is tied up in and so involved that one thinks that would stop you from going and living with anybody else because you'd always be thinking what it used to be like and perhaps you know if one had tried a bit more it could've worked and that stops me I suppose. And also the fact that, you know, I just, I love all my things. I'm terribly practical and material and I don't think I could really face the idea of a divorce or anything like that you know. But the thing that upsets me I suppose is that I really do want to be faithful to somebody because I only want one man and I just can't be faithful to Ben, because he's not faithful to me, and I'm sort of going against what I want.

NELL But this whole business of unfaithfulness is strange really because at the same time you yourself wouldn't really think that it was right to fall in love with one man at the beginning of your life and stay with him the whole of your life. Would you?

ANTONIA Well, Ben says that if you love somebody enough you should love them whatever they do so that if they fell in love with somebody else or wanted to go to bed with somebody else you'd still love them for it. Which I'm just incapable of doing. That's really very romantic bosh but I can see that perhaps one should be able to love enough.

NELL I think that if someone hurts you too much you stop loving them. I think the pain burns out the love.

However, I do think that if they then can be nice to you again they can resurrect the love but I think that while somebody's really torturing you you can't.

ANTONIA Well, the trust goes and you daren't, you just daren't expose yourself to reality, to their love, and Ben is being very nice to me now. But I don't believe it, you know, I really don't just believe it!

NELL What do you mean you don't believe it, you think it's just because he's in a good mood?

ANTONIA Yes, and if I'm miserable he'll win me round but then he'll drop me like a hot cake again —

NELL When he thinks you're alright he drops you?

ANTONIA Or you know, when his mood changes. And I'm all miserable again then. I know it — we're just in a very awkward position because I'm neurotic because I'm insecure so I'm not really myself and also he's sort of got me into a state where I'm absolutely too dependent on him, for love, he's sort of — I don't know what I'm trying to say really — he's just made me so insecure that I'm incapable of being sane about it. In the past one — you don't question the love, it's all taken for granted and one is sort of perfectly happy but when something happens like it did, I'm all the time looking, seeing petty things and thinking 'he doesn't love me' and he's really probably not thinking about loving me or not.

NELL Yes, one becomes over-aware of everything and I think what is particularly difficult for you is you've got nothing — you're insecure in every way, you're insecure in where you live, you're insecure financially, and you're insecure about the person you're living with, you don't know exactly when he's going to turn up. There's nothing that you've got absolutely secure in your life. I think this is tremendously hard for you but I think when you have the baby this will make a great difference although practically it will be even harder because you've two mouths to feed.

ANTONIA Well, one of the things I felt about having the baby was that I thought he was going to leave me and I thought 'well if I have a baby I won't need him', you know. Really, that's all I want. And I still feel that in a way, I'm terribly sort of dependent on him now, but once I've had it . . . I think he's very bad at carrying the load of anybody's depression, that's what you said to me once, I think it's very true.

NELL On the other hand he doesn't mind taking responsibility?

ANTONIA Well, he says he minds but I often wonder what he'd do without them. He'd be lost, you know, he says he's always fighting towards his freedom but he just gets more and more involved. This business about carrying depression – I think that men can't bear it when their women are unhappy or depressed because they expect them to be stronger emotionally. They always go down with you if you're depressed but if he's depressed I always try and pull him up – I never succeed, I always go down too but I think men can't bear it really when their women are unhappy. I think depression is like a disease anyway, sort of like leprosy. And you should try and be alone if possible.

NELL How important do you think sex is?

ANTONIA It's vastly important to me. If I'm frustrated I'm so incapable of doing anything. I feel unloved if I'm frustrated. I love making love so much, it's one of the nicest things there is. And so I attach vast importance to it.

NELL But I think this can build up to great resentment too if the man that you love doesn't make love to you.

ANTONIA I think it undermines your confidence. Some people express themselves physically and some don't. Ben just doesn't. And I like making love and so it's – this is

118

another vicious thing to me.

NELL I think it's an enormous thing because I think if you're being made love to everything else is small beside it, and you can manage, because there is this sort of –

ANTONIA I think it gives your whole life another dimension and it makes me love people more if I make love to them.

NELL It's a very complicated thing too because if one isn't being made love to it also makes sex rather unimportant therefore one can get on with all the other things much better. And I think this involves very much what you say like wanting to be faithful to one man, because I think that, one comes to a certain time in one's life when one wants to do all the things one wants to do and not spend one's life on street corners waiting for someone. One wants to live with one's lover.

ANTONIA It's only another language really. To me it's the way of communication that means the most to me, it means much more than words, it's much more convincing. Basically I'm terribly insecure and it just does so much to one's confidence.

NELL Is it rather appalling to think that eventually we're going to become unattractive?

ANTONIA Well, I just never really think about it because I – it's such a horrible thought really, like dying.

NELL Yes, but then think of all the lovely, all the spare time you'll have for reading and painting.

ANTONIA I'd get terribly bored with painting and reading if there was nothing else. Perhaps one's appetite changes and one sort of –

NELL They say it gets worse.

ANTONIA My God, it should be hell then. I'll jump out of the window. Growing old frightens me because I've seen so few old people who've got any serenity or who seem to have lived the sort of lives from which they've benefited. And most people seem so lonely. And so desperate. That frightens me. And so over the past few years I've felt a sort of frenzy in doing everything, experiencing anything, just for the hell of it, to learn from it. And getting myself into the most terrible situations just because I'm so frightened of not doing enough while I'm young and able to.

NELL How much do you live instinctively and how much according to plan?

ANTONIA I'm not at all impulsive really. I'd like to be. I often react impulsively and then think before I act and I'm very practical and sometimes if – I'd like to do something dramatic or – the instinctive thing to do, I'll think first and then do something entirely the opposite and very practical because I know that that's more intelligent but I think perhaps instinctive things are right. The Chinese think that one should react instinctively, don't they?

NELL I don't know, do they?

ANTONIA Somebody told me this. They don't believe in logic. They cut that out entirely and just act impulsively. They follow the heart. They must get in the most awful muddles.

NELL Do you feel you know the difference between right and wrong?

ANTONIA Not according to the way other people seem to think. I'm always being criticised for the things I do, being irresponsible and everybody thinks I'm very gullible. But I don't think it really matters what's right and what's wrong. I think you should just do what you want to do, as long as you're not going to hurt anyone.

NELL Well, that's the great thing isn't it, not to hurt anyone? But you don't feel that you had a definite moral code, like not sleeping with a married man?

ANTONIA I don't think it makes any difference really except that if anyone slept with Ben I'd get very angry.

NELL Could you sleep with a married man whose wife you knew well?

ANTONIA I think I'd feel guilty if she knew about it. Not if she didn't. I don't know. I mean I – because one's married one conventionally shouldn't sleep with anybody else. I'm always surprised when people think one shouldn't. I'm always surprised when you're criticised.

NELL But do people criticise you?

ANTONIA One feels that one is criticised by some people. In fact the reason why one doesn't discuss it, not because it's particularly – well it might be private – but because people won't approve really. One says one doesn't give a damn what people think but you do really.

NELL What about jealousy?

ANTONIA I think it's terribly bad to be jealous because it destroys so much. It's something that is uncontrollable, I find. I get terribly jealous when I think there's anything really in a relationship. I've always given Ben a reasonable amount of freedom and pretended not to care. Then something important happens and you get jealous about everything and it just spreads and completely undermines you.

NELL Then again, it's very bound up with sex because if they're involved with someone else and sleeping with someone else, they're not going to sleep with you, are they?

ANTONIA There is that, but I find I'm jealous over – whether he sleeps with them or not. I'm possibly more jealous because – just of the spiritual relationship.

NELL I don't think I'm jealous of spiritual relationships, I'm only jealous of physical ones.

ANTONIA Ben is very odd in a way, physically, and he

has this sort of warped idea about it being wrong to make love to somebody you love. So I feel if he doesn't make love to somebody who he's very fond of it's a sort of –

NELL What kind of things do you find erotic?

ANTONIA I find things to do with girls much more stimulating than boys. In fact I don't find men at all stimulating, unless they're close, touching you. I'm not a lesbian or anything like that but I just think girls are much more attractive than men. I have never yet fallen for a man because of his looks or anything like that, it's got nothing to do with looks. It's just the sort of aura I think isn't it? The sort of thing you set up between you.

NELL I don't know what it is, I just don't know. I think that it can go on because of looks because they're something to do, if you're bored as hell with them at least you can look at them! That's something. But tell me more about eroticism, does it play any part in your life?

ANTONIA Only if I'm frustrated actually. I get terribly worked up about symbolic things rather like that, and I find pictures of sexy girls erotic. I find wearing a black bra or something like that very erotic. I like silk pants because I like the feel of them.

NELL Because they're all slippery?

ANTONIA They're very sensual. Eroticism – being provoked by something sexy plays quite a big part in my life actually, I find. I go in cycles where I'm stimulated very easily by seeing things, movements, shapes, how people sit, just how one feels about somebody else I find stimulating. It also makes one want to feel close to them and perhaps touch them, and then other times I don't give a damn.

NELL But what about sensuality, do you feel it's the same sort of thing?

ANTONIA Yes and also it's a sort of atmosphere that one

can set up. I think sensuality is actually a more intimate thing isn't it? You can be made to feel erotic by something quite remote like going into a shop and seeing something you find erotic. Sensuality is much more human. In fact it's always got to do with flesh.

NELL The way people smell and all that sort of thing.

ANTONIA I find I'm terribly inhibited I think, sexually. Because I'd like to do so many things that I just daren't do. Because I feel one might be considered perverted. I'd just love to sleep with a man and another girl but I never have done.

NELL Do you think that many people are terribly inhibited because of the way they've been brought up?

ANTONIA Yes, I think not so much one's own circle of friends because I think most of my friends are fairly uninhibited but I think it's one thing wrong with the country, everybody's frustrated. Not everybody but a lot of people are, not doing half the things that they'd like to do, sexually. It comes out in so many ways, all the smutty conversations that go on and beastliness and dirtiness – pornography and things like this.

NELL But I remember a man once saying to me: 'Well my wife doesn't satisfy me, she's not sensual enough.' So I said: 'Well you're the only man she's had, why didn't you teach her?' And he said: 'Everybody's only got a certain height of – or depth of eroticism and you can't teach them more, you can't teach them sensuality.' Do you think this?

ANTONIA I think you can teach them through love.

NELL I think if a man gives you really physical confidence by his love-making, you can do anything. I think being inhibited is very much bound up with lack of physical confidence.

ANTONIA Yes, I think it is really. It's all to do with how convincing his love-making is, whether you feel he's just

satisfying himself or whether he wants to give you something. Because if you make love and you have felt that it
really has been making love, one feels so good afterwards
and can do anything.

NELL You feel someone really likes your body too. And
you can tell this very much with women, the way they
move, I think. If you had that sort of confidence it gives
you tremendous beauty. Everything. Dignity.

ANTONIA And if you don't, you shrivel up and become
– you probably wear twinsets and pearls.

NELL Do you think promiscuity is a good thing?

ANTONIA I've never really known what is meant by
promiscuity.

NELL Promiscuity means sleeping with anyone you
meet on the underground who you fancy.

ANTONIA Well, for me it's definitely wrong. Because
I'd be very unhappy being like that. I also feel that – well
I just can't make love to anybody like that. I have to get
to know them and like them, and have a definite love for
them. I think there're some people for whom this is the
only way.

NELL I can't help feeling this is rather odd because if it's
really good then why don't they want it again? It seems to
me it can't be very good otherwise they'd have a second
time and the third time therefore there wouldn't be another person because you'd still be with the same person.

ANTONIA Perhaps it's because people get desperate and
they're always looking for somebody, that is the only way
for them ever to get the right person. I think it's difficult
because you just wear yourself out emotionally. I suppose
I have in the past been fairly promiscuous, and I just get so
unhappy. When I slept with a lot of people I lost myself.
I lost my identity, and I didn't know where I was. I just
wanted to build myself up with somebody else really. I

don't think that perhaps it's an intelligent way to go about doing things because it means that you're always depending on somebody else, but love matters to me more than anything, so I can't be entirely independent. I'm bound to be deeply involved with somebody, in order to be happy. I think possibly it's not a very intelligent way to go about it. If it does wear out you're going to be left with nothing. This is why I want something. I want a job or some sort of interest that you can always fall back on.

NELL But it's falling back on it, rather than dedicating your life to it?

ANTONIA Yes. I dedicate my life to love really, to loving somebody. That's what I want. I don't want a career or anything like that. It bores me. I'd get terribly disinterested in things if I didn't belong. I've got no perseverance at all. If I take a job I'm bored within about two weeks. If I stick it for two months it's about as long as I can go on with anything. Because I really want to be at home, doing things at home, pottering around.

NELL Do you like being in the state of what's known as 'in love'?

ANTONIA Well, I'm a bit sceptical about it now but I used to. It used to be – the nice thing about it is that you're on your toes, it makes you feel very alive and aware of everything.

NELL It can, or it can have the effect of making the times when you're not with that person just kind of dead, because you're always waiting for the telephone or waiting for them. And you're always thinking about them and wasting a lot of time.

ANTONIA I think when it has happened to me, I'm completely unaware of everything except that person, so actually it is a sort of dead time as regards all one's other sort of interests, but I think it can be a very sort of magical time. And very moving really. It never lasts long. It's one of the things to learn that it's never going to last and you get so sceptical and I don't think I'll ever feel it again for anybody. I might do.

NELL How many times do you think you have been in love then?

ANTONIA About three, four times, I suppose.

NELL Why did you get married instead of living with Ben?

ANTONIA Only because of my parents, and because of the church. Because they were going to evict us. I got so fed up with lying about where I was living and the fact that it would hurt them if they – well, my father not so much because I think he knew although we never discussed it but it would've just hurt my mother so much. And I was just fed up with pretending. I had no other reasons for getting married. Marriage didn't mean to me what I suppose it means to a lot of people. It does now in a way, when I'd like to leave Ben because I'm unhappy with him, I do try especially because I'm married to him. Because he's my husband and it does give it depth, but it didn't at the time. I mean I had no motives for getting married other than that. But definitely now I'm more deeply involved because I'm married to him, than I would've been if I'd still lived the same period with him.

NELL It would've just been an affair. It's rather appalling how much attention people do pay to it, actually finally everyone is always on the side of the wife. Do you live more in the present than in the past or the future?

ANTONIA I think I live very much in the present and in the past. I don't think about the future much. I suppose I do more now because I think of the baby and things to do with the baby growing up, you know, but on the whole I think I live terribly in the present and that's why

I can't bear it if — we've just moved and I can't bear it being so chaotic and horrible there now, whereas Ben it doesn't worry him at all because in his mind it's what it's going to be, already done and he's living in it like that but I'm living in it as it is with packing cases all round me, and the floorboards half up and things. But I don't think about the future much at all. I never have thought of the future. I think about the past a lot and I'm always absolutely amazed at the path my life has taken really and I can't think it's me.

NELL When you were young did you imagine the kind of life you would have?

ANTONIA I was terribly ordinary, much more ordinary than I am now. I lived with my mother in North London and I never had much experience of how different one's life — people's lives — are. I suppose I just imagined getting married and having children and living a very ordinary life. And I suppose I would've done that if I hadn't met various people at a very influential age.

NELL Do you in any way regret not having that ordinary life?

ANTONIA Oh no, not at all. No, I'm so grateful to Ben really showing me that one can lead a different sort of life to the one one's been brought up to and I'm going terribly against my parents all the time. And I feel this, as a sort of thorn in a way. I find that sometimes I'm doing something and I change what I'm doing because I think of my father, influenced by what he'd like and much more now as I feel he's getting older and I want to please him. And it's awful really because it means that one is going against oneself.

NELL It's awful when one is torn between one's father and husband.

ANTONIA Yes, well this is my conflict I suppose and I'm going more with my father now because I think he's old, he's getting old. I suppose I'm a bit sentimental because Ben's father just died and Ben was upset because he hadn't made much effort towards his father. I think people are terribly cruel to their parents. So many people I know just don't care. And really I'm so fond of my father although I've had a lot to criticise him for. And I always regret being very remote from my mother. I'd like to be close to her but I can never understand why I'm not.

NELL Are you interested at all in politics?

ANTONIA I'm not at all. I feel terribly ashamed of myself, I don't understand politics. I think terribly few women are interested in politics and I find them too objective. I think I'm terribly selfish, inasmuch as I'm only interested in things that directly involve me.

NELL But do you have any sense of duty?

ANTONIA I do towards individuals. I can never get too involved with masses or an ideal or anything like that, it's too remote. I feel I have a sense of duty towards John for instance who is incapable.

NELL That's very interesting really because I'm the opposite. I can see things from a sort of plane of right and wrong, socialism and things, I'm not really interested in helping individuals. The people I am moved by are working-class people who work their guts out all their lives and never ask for pity. The people who are washed up through weakness, individual weakness, I don't seem to be moved by.

ANTONIA I feel that I wouldn't get involved again with somebody like John. So I say I get involved with individuals, not that it's really through choice, it's just that when they come your way I always feel that it's very difficult to turn people away.

NELL I feel a duty towards my friends in that if one has a bond of friendship with someone and they're in need one should do what one can to help them.

ANTONIA Yes, I think you're quite right there. I always get terribly upset if someone I know closely is hurt or ill or something like that but I think I haven't got much sense of duty, except towards people I'm involved with. I don't care about many people, just a handful I really care about. If I see somebody knocked over in the road, and I don't know them, I feel a bit strange but I don't get upset.

NELL I know one thing that interests me very much that you were saying the other day that when you were pregnant by someone you weren't in love with the idea of having a child didn't appeal to you.

ANTONIA It didn't. I think I said I would have killed him, I think I would. I would have hated it.

NELL Do you know why at all?

ANTONIA Well, as soon as I got pregnant I felt I hated this person, I couldn't bear the sight of him, I couldn't bear his face, I thought you know, a child growing up and looking like him and having the same eyes or the same mouth I just couldn't bear it. Actually now I still see him and I like him again, it's alright.

NELL Have you not been able to sleep with him since that time?

ANTONIA Oh no, I couldn't go near him.

NELL That's amazing.

ANTONIA He just leaves me cold.

NELL And you were in love with him until this happened?

ANTONIA I was terribly in love with him and absolutely so in harmony, it was really incredible.

NELL Physical harmony?

ANTONIA And mental harmony.

NELL Then why didn't you want his child?

ANTONIA I still wanted Ben as well you see.

NELL You were in love with Ben, really, and that would

have finished it with him wouldn't it?

ANTONIA Yes. Absolutely, as you said the other day, you thought it would've been a threat to my life with Ben, which it would've been. And I would have felt terribly at a disadvantage if Ben had accepted somebody else's child, I'd never have a leg to stand on! But I don't think it was quite as simple as that. I really hated the thing.

NELL And yet you had a great desire to have a child?

ANTONIA Yes, I wanted to have one terribly. And yet I just couldn't bear that I was carrying that thing around in me, I felt physically sick. And I didn't feel any guilt at having an abortion, I just felt such a relief. It was so marvellous not to be pregnant any more.

NELL But do you think that if you'd got pregnant and it was just once you slept with him and nobody knew, and nobody would have known, you would still have wanted to get rid of it?

ANTONIA Well, I think I would because I'm – I couldn't keep a secret like that, I'm hopeless. I would've told Ben. I think because I couldn't live with it.

NELL You're not a secretive person really?

ANTONIA Not at all. I can't – I always feel that it might be an advantage to be able to keep things to oneself, especially like that for instance, but I couldn't. I'm getting better at it now, but basically I'm not. It's something perhaps one learns.

NELL I think it isn't, I think it's in temperament, I think if one has a rather sly, mysterious kind of temperament, one finds it easy to tell lies and to keep a secret.

ANTONIA I don't lie much at all.

NELL I know I started lying out of necessity because I was unable to tell people certain things. This is this whole thing of hypocrisy, I learned as a child I couldn't admit things because it wouldn't have been acceptable.

ANTONIA Well, I think lying anyway is just purely a reflection of what you think of the other person, or what you think they can accept or not accept.

NELL Yes, but do you have a sort of image of yourself as how you'd like people to see you?

ANTONIA Yes, I think I do in an idealistic sort of way and I know it's completely the opposite to what I am.

NELL How?

ANTONIA Well, I think I like to be thought to be attractive, and successful without being a career woman or anything like that. Just sort of good at what I was doing, and entertaining and witty which I'm not a bit. I'd love to be, I'd love people to think I was funny but I've got no sense of humour at all. Well I have in a way, but not my own, I'm not original in my witticisms. I don't often see the funny side of things unless it's pointed out to me and then I find things terribly funny, but I'd like to be thought that I was witty. I think I should like to be thought of as highly efficient which I'm not. And practical and getting things done. Whereas actually it takes me a long time to get anything done, to get round to doing things, and I find I'm always perhaps leading people to believe that I'm efficient and – just getting things done.

NELL How about clever?

ANTONIA I'd like to be thought I was intelligent, or perhaps more intuitive. But I'm not at all. Well, I am in a way, inasmuch as I can see people quite well but I'm not clever in the accepted sense. Another thing I'd like people to think is that I'm aggressive and fierce, which I'm not a bit, I'm very passive.

NELL I like people to think that about me, it's a way of protecting oneself.

ANTONIA It's a way of making people think that you get things done and that you feel deeply about things.

And also that you're – they can't get at you. One is more aloof, I like to be a bit aloof and not somehow enter in too much. This is one of the things – one of the reasons – why I in some respects lead a very masculine sort of life, to build the house, and like getting dirty and with blow-lamps, things like that. Because I think it makes me look fierce. It's mad.

NELL It's also physical, isn't it?

ANTONIA Yes I suppose it is. You're quite right, it does give one the sort of armour. Aggression. I'm not a bit aggressive really. I used to like riding my scooter because it used to make me feel aggressive, seem aggressive, if I'd do it fast, which was absolute nonsense.

NELL Does the idea of freedom mean anything to you?

ANTONIA No, it doesn't at all. Not at the moment. Living with Ben it doesn't, particularly. I've got as much freedom, more freedom than I want with Ben. I wish – this sort of business of personal freedom – I'd like him to be more possessive about me. On the other hand if I lived with someone who was more possessive, I'd hate it.

NELL Do you think you'd like Ben to say: 'Yes, well, let's have supper at 7 o'clock every evening and spend the evening together, you get my supper ready and then we'll go to the pictures or stay in.' Something as regular as this?

ANTONIA Well, I might like it for a week as a change – it if it became a habit it would become boring.

NELL You don't think you'd like that? I rather like my daytimes to be free but have a sort of regular meeting place in the evening.

ANTONIA Really I couldn't imagine it with Ben. I couldn't ever see it coming off but . . . I think we have discussed things like this, that we'd spent two evenings a week at home together, they never happen like that. Something happens. I always have the weekends, that

we're always together. That's super. We always used to
in the old house always have Sunday, as a sort of day at
home and I'd cook a lunch at midday rather than something in the evening and we always had this American on
Sundays who used to help us in the house and I loved that,
and used to look forward to Sundays, and never make any
plans to do anything else and then that fizzled out and it's
never come back. We really don't spend too much time
together. If Ben is in evenings he's always busy writing
letters or something like that. We never really spend any
time doing anything together. And I would like to have,
say, one or two evenings a week just enjoying each other,
doing things. But because of bad organisation and other
things we've never done this really. I feel now that I'm not
interested enough in Ben to want to spend as much time
with him.

NELL But does he say to you: 'I'll be back at such and
such a time?'

ANTONIA Well, he does sometimes but he doesn't
usually turn up. This doesn't worry me because I just cook
when he appears. Over the last week or two I've been getting lunch for him sometimes which I enjoyed doing, getting it ready at a certain time and he's come in and eaten
it and then gone out again. And I like, as you said, having
something as a map. I like having certain things to do at
certain times because it gives a sort of shape and pattern
to the day.

NELL It gives it rhythm.

ANTONIA I like to have the day free and cook in the
evening, but it just happened like this, Ben wants to eat at
midday at the moment. I find it upsets my day rather, because I'm very bad in the mornings, you know, I go round
with my eyes closed and can't concentrate on anything.
By the time I've had something to eat I feel half asleep

again. But I always used to work all day and I found being hungry a stimulant and I'd get more done. I can't work when I've eaten a lot. It sort of fogs you up. You want to lie down and read a book or shut your eyes or something.

NELL It's very hard to know how much of one's life – for instance sometimes I'm working and I suddenly feel I would like to lie on the sofa and read a book, then I say to myself, 'No, you must work,' I'd say: 'Well why, if I want to read a book, that's what I should be doing.' How much should one indulge oneself? This is a very tricky thing, how much? Which is exactly the same thing as promiscuity if one fancies someone, why exactly shouldn't one want sleep with them? It's difficult to know.

ANTONIA I indulge myself too much but I think the bitterness of denying can be equally bad. This is the way I was brought up in a Catholic school. One was constantly taught to deny oneself because it was good for your soul or something. I think it's absolute balls.

NELL But I find myself walking along the street and I pass a sweet shop and I think it would be nice to have a piece of chocolate. When I go in and buy the chocolate and eat it and in a way I feel pleased at giving myself this very simple pleasure of eating a bar of chocolate and I feel the world is full of good little things.

ANTONIA I indulge myself by staying in bed late. It's also a terrific escape because I can't face things but I argue about whether I'm just going to lie in bed or lie and read. If I lie in bed and read I'm going to stay in bed much longer. I'm not going to put the book down and sometimes I allow myself to do that and when I do get up I feel so guilty I think it's ridiculous. I've indulged myself without enjoying it really. Because I feel guilty afterwards. If one does other things like allowing oneself to have an affair with somebody or anything like that, invariably I find that one comes out in the end none the better for it. You come out feeling guilty, so I don't know, I think you should let yourself do things you *really* want to do, I love lying down having a sleep when I'm tired.

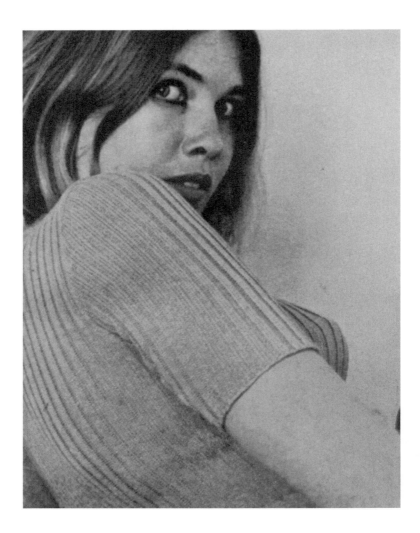

SUNA

Twenty-four

NELL Why did you start writing and painting?

SUNA I don't feel I started, I feel as though I always have done. It's a peculiar sort of itch. I have a real need, a tactile need to take hold of things by solidifying them, either in paint or words.

NELL To make some meaning out of life?

SUNA In a way it's that but it's not only that. One can say afterwards there is this thing of wanting to chronicle everything so therefore I exist more because I've written about that. But there is the moment when you feel you want to write or to paint because you want to. It's got to be out of you and it's got to be put down. Writing is the most involving and wonderful because it carries you on for many months, it's marvellous to do a piece of writing, to know that the next day you're going to continue with that which is frightfully difficult even impossible at the moment and yet it makes a wonderful sort of continuum, all brightness and on the levelness, you couldn't die at those times.

NELL What I like about the way you write is it gives one the feeling that the texture of life is enough, eating and being and loving and sex, this marvellous physical world.

Do you think this is what life is about?

SUNA Yes, but that's sort of living in the moment. I do believe in being like that if you possibly can. But the thing is to make the fabric of the moment as rich as possible and that does involve thinking about it and not letting yourself drift. You've got to have some ideas about what the moment should be – the sort of atmosphere in which you want to be involved, before you embark upon being in it. There's got to be a definite discrimination about what you do before you do it. If you talk about a hedonistic world as the enjoyment of all sorts of lovely things, the sun and eating and lying around, and making love and working in a pleasant way and all that kind of thing, it doesn't just fall in your lap.

NELL And has your life got better?

SUNA It's got much better.

NELL Because it's fuller?

SUNA It is just rather relieving to know more. When you're very young, when all sensations are new it's quite alarming, but when you can parallel it with things that went before it's not so bad. And you know very much better how to make your own life more pleasant for yourself and probably for other people. I think that's a danger as a matter of fact too. The older you become the better you become at making life sort of nice and that in itself can be rather deadening because less unexpected things happen.

NELL Yes, in some ways that's so but in another way I find that I can say 'Right, I'll go out and just something might happen, and I'm not frightened of that happening.' I can let something happen to myself whereas before I was so vulnerable that I couldn't let anything happen to myself that I didn't choose to happen.

SUNA No, I don't think that. I think absolutely the opposite. I think that one gets conditioned and you know the sort of thing that can happen to you after a while, one is less prepared for the real adventure the older you get.

NELL Do you think life's primarily a tragic thing that we've got to make the best of?

SUNA Yes, I do. I feel all the time that the only way people are really happy is that they've built up castles in their mind literally of: 'This is the person. This is the way of life. This is the job,' whatever it is, and they fit everything that's going on around them into their sort of mould. They say: 'Yes, that's him, he's doing something funny' in fact, it all fits in with a plan, as it were. It's all illusion and suddenly sometimes it breaks down and one suddenly feels rather ill and one looks clearly and realises that one's made one's own vision of the world – we regulate our eyes to such a horrible extent . . .

NELL Do you think we should set any store by the past? Because you've lost someone should it really matter or should we just move on to the next thing?

SUNA I don't think you should set any store by it, no. I think you should be grateful.

NELL Are girls the ones that decide things emotionally?

SUNA Yes. They do, yes. I mean any girl who is a proper girl in her own right does decide what goes on. I really long to meet a man who is as definite as a woman and yet still a man, but I've never met anybody who was like that, ever.

NELL You mean they're not whole in quite the same way as women?

SUNA Men always have to be sort of told in the end, what's going on, what the atmosphere is.

NELL Do you think you've chosen the men in your life or they've chosen you?

SUNA I'm afraid I think I've chosen them. Although I don't want it to be like that.

NELL Why should you not want it to be like that?

SUNA I just want it the opposite way round, I think that I do anyway. I think that I'd like to be completely taken over in a way although I know I'd absolutely hate it.

NELL Choosing is awfully tiring in a way.

SUNA No, I don't think it's tiring, to me it's completely inevitable. I'm never consciously choosing though I suppose initially one is, if you know what the sort of people or the thing that you'd like all you can do is make every effort to get nearer to it.

NELL Don't you think the thing is to find a man who's both physically attractive and mentally appealing?

SUNA Yes, but really the physical attraction is the most important thing of all. You're ready to put up with things, from somebody you find physically attractive, to a sort of tenfold extent. One doesn't want to hear the most brilliant things constantly when it comes to living with people.

NELL I think one of the important things about people is that they should be whole, rather than brilliant.

SUNA Yes, exactly. But what worries me is wanting very much to admire people. And it's terrible once you've given your admiration, once you've said: 'Well that's what you are and that's my relation to you' then to be either bored or uninterested or to think: 'Well, you're not so admirable as I thought you originally were.' That's rather difficult to reconcile yourself to. On the other hand it happens.

NELL Do you ever get this thing of wanting to be admired yourself? Rather than loved?

SUNA Not any more, now I'm only interested in someone that I want to talk to or whatever it's all about, before, I always used to be wanting to impress.

NELL I think the sort of thing about impressing is that it is a kind of protection for oneself. If you can impress people you somehow push them away a bit.

SUNA Yes, that's true. It also gives you terrific leeway, you can say or do anything if you know they're receiving you and interested in you and that kind of thing, whatever you do, it gives you a wonderful freedom. You gain confidence by people's interest in you. When people have decided that somebody's rather marvellous and enjoy being with them they'll give tenfold as it were. And they'll be far more accepting too, the whole thing is exaggerated. That's what liking people is, I suppose. Exaggerating something you originally liked about them.

NELL It suddenly occurred to me that one doesn't really know what's right and wrong.

SUNA You mean morally? I've absolutely no idea at all. I've never had any kind of idea about it at all. I don't know what's right or wrong. If you had an affair with a married man obviously from the world's point of view and probably from hers it's wrong, but on the other hand maybe she's having an affair with somebody else too. Maybe they're desperately unhappy, or maybe it's making him the most possibly happy.

NELL Then why is it wrong to have an affair with a married man?

SUNA You're breaking up social convention.

NELL Yes, but then why is it wrong to break up social convention?

SUNA It's not, surely. It's so dead.

NELL I think I know of some things being wrong. Like really wilfully hurting people who are defenceless and things.

SUNA I think all sorts of nasty moods against other people which are thought out beforehand, I think that's wrong.

NELL Have you ever tried to work out any ethics for living or do you just act instinctively really?

SUNA I only ever write lists for myself, like 'read more' and 'concentrate harder', that sort of thing.

NELL You used to live abroad. Does the sun help you work?

SUNA No, it's very bad for work because it has this thing of hitting you on the head, and numbing you. I love the sun and I love the way it makes you expand like after sex but I'm longing for the evening all day long in fact, the darkness, the moment when one can think.

NELL In the long run it cuts you off from yourself.

SUNA It's a real addiction you know.

NELL Do you daydream?

SUNA I used to do that the whole time, I used to live entirely in the future but the thing about young people is that they are always thinking about the next thing, they're always looking forward to their future rather than living in the present. I feel now that I'm living in the present and I don't look into the future at all. I can't think for myself very much any longer. When I was with Bill I was just longing for the time when I'd do this or that, when I'd left him. I suppose it's a question of one's life becoming enough. If you become responsible in a sense for somebody else because you really care about them, then it's just a question of what happens to you both next. Though I often write things about how I should be in the future when I read something which inspires me. 'That's how it will be all the time, I've got to do this.' A sort of way of being. And one writes it down.

NELL One thing Pauline said is that she'd like her life to be in a state of chaos. Do you feel this at all?

SUNA No, I don't. Because I don't see how you can think if there's a state of chaos. You're immediately put into a false position of working things out and everything's having terrific effects and all that. If you are very egoistic

142

and want to get on with your own things which is artistic things, writing, you've got to have a fairly calm background. I find one wants to do each thing separately each moment, one wants to read a book or paint a picture and give oneself to the picture, but it's boring being bugged the whole time by some worry: 'Is he going to turn up tonight?' – it just kind of bores me!

NELL Do you think that passion is an excuse for anything?

SUNA Well, feeling passionate about things is about the most important thing there is, but I don't think it is an excuse.

NELL Do you ever feel jealous?

SUNA Yes.

NELL How does it feel?

SUNA The most awful feeling in the whole world. I never felt jealous till I was with Bill and first of all I was jealous of his past. I absolutely had to emulate it, you know, I was jealous of his sexual past.

NELL But do you think the idea of sexual fidelity is complete hypocrisy, that it just can't exist? People always want other people after a certain amount of time?

SUNA I don't know about that. I'll write to you in about two years' time. I was very perturbed by a story I read today by D.H. Lawrence called 'St Mawr'. It's about a horse.

NELL A stallion?

SUNA A great big stallion.

NELL What happens?

SUNA He sort of symbolises life, and sex and everything to this rather bored smart American girl but her mother is the dominant character of all and she's – she's about fifty in the book, and she's given up men about twenty years ago and lives and is very interested in everything and definite about everything but really has given up on men.

Because they never came up to her standards, so-called. On the other hand she realises – Lawrence tells you a great deal – that every man or thing that she ever wanted she wanted to admire, you know, but at the same time she was really destroying them and she really wanted them to kiss her hand. Once she admired somebody, right, she'd build them right up rather than move away, but really what she was working for underneath was to make them be subservient to her. And she'd always managed to make it happen – it always had happened. And therefore she just sort of lost interest. Well that struck me very strongly. I feel rather identified with her. I wonder who she was based on? He's very extraordinary, Lawrence, one should read him all the time.

NELL Do you think that sex comes much more easily and is much more part of the thing when there's sun?

SUNA Yes, in a way. On the other hand once it becomes a way of life it gets tempered down in the way that anything else does.

NELL You get used to it?

SUNA It is certainly a more sexy atmosphere, immediately the sun shines now today in London suddenly you notice everybody and everybody else is noticing each other far more, partly they've got fewer clothes on or something. There's a sort of breath of sex in the air. Most of the time people are rushing about in overcoats and feeling rather miserable and hating each other – that's why they're so cold to one another. They just want to stay inside themselves and create some warmth inside themselves. There's no looking about and there's no sort of eyeing – it's a wonderful thing when the sun suddenly comes in London. It's really extraordinary – everyone looks entirely different.

NELL Do you worry about growing old?

SUNA I think about death terrifically much and I feel on the edge of it all the time, I feel just paper, skin and paper between me and death the whole time. And then it's fascinating at night walking to a square to watch children playing. The next day, somebody's died, and you knew them and had contact with them, now they're dead, now they've gone and that same thing could happen to you the next minute if you walked the wrong way too quickly. It's so there, but it doesn't really matter all that much.

NELL It matters to me if I wake up in the middle of the night and I feel death and I suddenly think what it would be like to be put in a coffin and one's body in the coffin and a great physical feeling I want to cling on to another human body because it feels warm and alive.

SUNA And that will go on giving you life.

NELL I just feel tremendously alone and lonely. And I have this terrible feeling that once dead one will be completely alone in this awful coffin, shut in.

SUNA No, I'm not going to have any coffin. I'm going to be burnt. I've always said that ever since I was five. I'm going to be scattered on Hod Hill – I'm certain I'll never get put in a coffin.

NELL I've never thought of that. Do you put it in your will?

SUNA Yes, just tell anybody now. It's important.

NELL You haven't actually written a will and put it in?

SUNA No, I've never written a will, but I've always told my mother and anybody I've ever been closest to in case anything frightful happened. I couldn't bear to be put in a coffin.

NELL What is it you were telling me earlier about experiencing things?

SUNA Well, just that whatever you write presumably has got to have some authenticity as it were, in your own

145

experience, I mean you've got to experience something or know the subject pretty well, haven't you? All the people you're talking about, all the action takes place, the way I write anyway, I just think myself back into a situation, it seems always to be autobiographical. If you just think of yourself, take a whole day that you remember quite well, even three years ago, and you know who's there, you know the sort of atmosphere and things that were going on. You can recreate it, different yet based on truth.

NELL But I can hardly even do that you know, I even have to do it more directly than that, I have to make notes almost, very shortly after. For instance I usually every morning before I do anything apart from getting up and having tea, is I write in my notebook, about things that have happened the day before. First thing in the morning. It's the first thing I do before I work or anything.

SUNA Can you always find something?

NELL No, sometimes I can't find anything to write. But then I'm using up past material. It's kind of like a bank book, paying in.

SUNA But can you find the bits that you want to find afterwards?

NELL Yes, I can because I've got very used to it, and I read through, and I stick in markers and also what I've always found is that my whole life springs together very closely because one is the central person and therefore in a way all material can get used in the same mill or a tremendous amount of it can. Occasionally I stick something in but then it all seems to come together when I'm writing something and sorting out all this material, and restringing it like a necklace. Putting the beads on in a certain order. But the initial thing is writing down things that have occurred to me. Or I've heard, or have happened. And this is what I was saying earlier, what does one do when one is leading a very cabbagey life?

SUNA The thought – sometimes when one has noticed a peculiar lot the night before, even the day before a lot's happened, but the thought of the energy to get it all down, in the end you need to get it all down, is absolutely whacking.

NELL I find the energy to sort it all out and to see that it's valid or to actually read it is enormous. I find the actual writing it down, creating as I go along, in phrases, and re-membering odd phrases and remembering the visual de-tails I really enjoy – in fact that's one of my most enjoyable things, that half hour at the beginning of the day between half past nine and ten or when I get away.

SUNA I've got lots of diaries, I've kept diaries, not at a set time, but then I get this awful obligation towards it. I feel I've left so much out since I last wrote it and that kind of thing, there's really no point in writing it now, because I've lost the chronology of the thing. It stops you writing in that book. So I'm much more apt to write on bits of paper, which is dodgier still, because one either loses them or else they're all so mucky. I thought today, I began to write, I wrote about six pages of my thoughts and the general situation as it were – that's how Virginia Woolf used to write her diary, on foolscap just like that and pin them together and not regularly either.

NELL The thing I find is that if one keeps these 'diaries' people are apt to have a thing about secrecy, are apt to read them, and it inhibits how one writes them. This is very bad. This of course is one of the great things about having my room because nobody goes to my room and I have my diary there. And this is very private. I have a great thing about privacy, I think it's terribly important. Because I think it allows oneself – I think why one is inhibited possibly a lot of the time is because one is so vulnerable. You can be completely yourself, no one can get at you. You can learn to be more yourself.

SUNA That's a very big thing against a diary, that I feel people are reading it.

NELL But I have it bare, my room, and I go off each morning there and write it in there. Lately of course I haven't been going there so much for one reason or another but I went there today and immediately I felt kind of liberated, 'this is mine, no one can get at me, I can write what I like' and I wrote masses in my diary because I haven't written – I've written terribly little for about two weeks so I've had it here and just made little bits each morning out of habit. I haven't really let myself go, I know no one can get at me there. It's a kind of space.

SUNA I think that is terribly important.

NELL It's lovely and the day stretches off – even if it's only till 1 o'clock it's time, that amount of time, four hours to be in this . . .

SUNA What is your room like? Is it in a house?

NELL It's in a house.

SUNA Can't you hear anything?

NELL No, one other person lives there, he's a painter and he's very quiet and I never hear him.

SUNA What sort of floor is there, has it got light and everything?

NELL Yes, it's lovely and looks over a railway, it's got a window, it's a tiny room but quite a big window. Just a table and chair and bed and filing cabinet. That's all.

SUNA Do you know something I thought the other day . . . just like training yourself to read in a roomful of people or something. I'm obviously going to have to work at home. I used to get into a frenzy, an absolute frenzy with someone about me, which if you let people see that you're annoyed by the fact that they intrude, it makes them do it

148

all the more. Just stifled me you know. I suddenly thought, well in fact people can't stop me writing. If I quietly go on, if I say I'm working there's nothing anyone can do except go off, so really if you could just count to ten and relax one can perfectly well carry on with your own secret life and diary and not let it get bugged, and not have to hide too much. One is hidden inside oneself really. I have to explain this to myself because I get so neurotic about the thing of being interrupted or . . .

NELL There's a terrible critical balance about how much one is prepared to sacrifice for one's work. I can't help always feeling that life is more important and therefore, for instance the thing of upsetting the person you love because you want to write is mad.

SUNA Absolutely. One feels, Oh hell one would be much better to be . . .

NELL Much better to be making a cup of coffee or something. Do you ever try and analyse why you love a certain person?

SUNA Well, I did used to think that one did love people for a reason, that they fitted in to one's not exactly 'ideal', but lots of things which all added up to, attraction, therefore making one love them. But really now I don't even attempt to analyse why.

NELL But does passion have a meaning?

SUNA Yes.

NELL What is it exactly?

SUNA Perhaps it's absolutely overboard sort of thing, go all the way, about something.

NELL Is this what one wants, do you think?

SUNA I think an element of passion is essential. To be with anybody I feel it's got to be terribly loaded.

NELL Sort of override all the irritating things? To make it all worthwhile. Why exactly does one live with someone instead of living on one's own?

SUNA I think it just is very much nicer to share the bulk of your life. One wants privacy and everything else but it is just a human need to feel that kind of warm background, a sort of knowledge that the person will be there, or will be there soon. That they're there in your life.

NELL But a lot of things have no meaning at all on one's own, I don't think, like a meal's got no meaning on one's own, for oneself.

SUNA No, but if you like doing that kind of thing which in fact I do, I rather like the domestic side of things, and things like that, creating, trying to create a nice life, making good food and all that kind of thing, and a nice comfortable atmosphere, having people and that sort of thing around you. When you like doing that you need people and you need an absolute counterpart.

NELL And I think probably this makes when you are alone more special. I find that after living here with people coming in and out a lot and children around that going to this room is something very kind of immaculate for me, I suddenly feel my mind is completely clean and what I think is in space, as opposed to being sandwiched between hearing somebody's voice and feeling sensations about them, and pleasure, and looking at the things one's made. To have this completely white room where one is, one's stripped off everything and you see very clearly what you want to write about.

NELL Do you find girls erotic?

SUNA What do you mean?

NELL Does erotic mean anything to you? I'm not quite sure what it means. I think it means visual sensations of sex.

SUNA I think it's a capacity that any person, not girls particularly, a man or a woman has, of feeling and expressing — I mean they're stimulated, right, but how deeply that actually registers upon them enables them to respond erotically, that's what I call a measure of eroticism. It's fairly rare now, isn't it? I mean in normal people's lives there are so many other things, like jobs and . . . They haven't got time and they haven't got the measure. Or just daring or just the effort. I think that — well obviously it takes place at different times in your life, you can have a very erotic time for a long period and then perhaps not at all, you might be very interested in doing something else and not spending your energy in that way. It is purely to do with sex, isn't it?

NELL Yes I think so, but I think it's sex on an inactive plane. Finding things exciting through looking at them or thinking about them but passively.

SUNA Yes I see what you mean. But I think that's just your interpretation of the world. I think eroticism is a thing, isn't it? An actual active thing.

NELL Is it?

SUNA Oh yes, I think so. I mean one's got to have either visual stimulation or physical stimulation. It's really basic, I feel that it's completely from inside, sort of . . . vibrations.

NELL Where do you feel you write from? When you're really enjoying writing you're in it, what part of you, physically do you feel involved?

SUNA That's interesting because it's as if one is drawing out from two or three places and it becomes a place here that you're writing from. If you're writing from your head, it's no good. If you're writing almost from your sex or inside, again it's no good and it's got to be a moment when these two join and that's the moment when everything comes right. I always used to think it was a very odd thing because it seemed to come from somewhere you didn't know about and one seemed to be writing things that one didn't know, but what I finally realised was that it's in those rare moments when one's spirit and one's body join up that it goes.

NELL And that is the creative thing I think. Everything comes together. And therefore you're writing things you didn't know about because those moments are so rare. That's what's so marvellous, that's why the feeling is so terribly good, the feeling of creating. Because you're using every inch of yourself. That's why it's so exhausting too. Everything makes sense. I think one doesn't try hard enough, in fact it's one of my complaints. I don't try hard enough, because one hasn't the space in one's life. As I say, I have to get into that room and be there for about an hour probably before I can start working, also to know that everything is alright at home, there's food in the house, and that I haven't got to hurry back too early then I can – if all the things are right I can work. But at the same time it's an awful lot of effort making all these things right so half the time one doesn't bother. What is it that makes one bother? You know, one is at home, messing about, sticking things in books and drinking cups of tea and talking to Roc, well, why on earth should one bother to write?

SUNA I know, it's very strange the urge to do so. It's very encouraging to me that you go on writing, you're still absolutely in it, having had children and having a complete life around you. Sometimes I think if I had a child perhaps I would never want to write any more, create any more, but I don't think that's true. I think there is a certain type of person who has always got this kind of itch, maybe it's a sort of maladjustment or something really lacking in one that one needs to create further if one is to enlarge one's life. To me it's the only time I'm really alive, creating.

NELL I think it is something and I feel it you know, even

today, having gone to the room, I haven't for the last three or four days, haven't gone for the whole of the week, this is the first day I've gone. I've been doing bits and pieces. And it's just a completely different feeling being there, I forget how much I love it, how much myself I feel and how much away I feel from all the sort of petty things like buying cabbage, which is lovely and fine but one needs this other thing so much, one needs to try and draw some sort of essence, make some sense out of it all.

SUNA And if you find, what I find very much indeed, is that it makes me able if I'm working and I'm really involved with my own thoughts, I can have a certain amount of time for work, it makes the whole of the rest of my life, all the petty things I have to do like buying food, very very much easier, more relaxed. I don't get irritated with other people, I think that well that's the way they're going on and I just don't get bugged because I've got this basic thing behind me. Of my own work. It's wonderful that, and if I stop working I find I get so neurotic over cooking a meal, over irritations. It emphasises everything so much if I haven't got my own thing going on. One feels one's life is being eaten up by these petty things, you become totally involved with them instead of involved in something really wider. After the first flush of sex one wants to settle down into a life and have all the other things. And that's why it's hopeless having an affair with somebody who's married. Because you can't have those nice cosy things with them.

NELL Is it terribly different living alone from living with someone? Does your life take on a totally different pattern?

SUNA Yes. I think one becomes desperately pernickety and selfish about your own particular little habits and very intolerant of people bursting in on you, or the unexpected happening. That sort of thing happens all the time when you're living with somebody and you grow to accept that and you adjust yourself to it. But if for a large part of the time you're alone it just does make one like an old maid, habits and things.

NELL Do you have any religious feelings?

SUNA No, not really. It's rather awful really because I had it killed by Bill. I used to be really quite religious, and he so completely didn't believe in God and he was at the time so much the person that I believed, and he ridiculed the whole thing so much, and said in absolute rational terms what one deeply suspected that there wasn't a God, that it was quite illusory and so much of the church was a con anyway and it was so obvious that it's a human need for something bigger than ourselves, it seemed to be silly to go on conning oneself just because you've been taught to. Maybe one will become religious again, I'd have to be absolutely convinced, all over again.

NELL One of the things religion tries to do is make out a definite meaning of life, rather than have to make one's own meaning.

SUNA Yes, it rather does it for you, doesn't it? I don't believe that. I think one must make one's own meaning. It's too easy this thing to rely on.

NELL But does the thing of mysticism mean anything in your life? Stars and fate and that kind of thing?

SUNA Yes, a lot and the other thing that means a great deal to me is this thing that is all very bound up with people and psychology but not coincidence. I don't believe in coincidence, but the strange sort of psychic contact between people, between events and even objects, the strange sort of connection that can be made all the time.

NELL I think you're terribly strong on this, because you take terribly quickly against people or for them don't you? In a very psychic way almost. Do you know at all about this, why you do?

SUNA Well, I think it's just probably chemical and I express it. If one meets somebody who quite obviously grates against yourself, I just don't want to know. I'm rather aggressive about it, I don't want them to come anywhere near me at all.

NELL In fact I think one of the great things about not having a job and keeping oneself, one keeps oneself rather aloof and therefore kind of fresh to people. But if you've been kind of worn against people all the time, all the day, it would be exhausting.

SUNA And another thing too is this awful sort of moulding into a character. You have to be the character that they all think you are, all the time.

NELL Why, because it's such a strain not to be, you mean?

SUNA Well, they'd be so surprised if you weren't. But people do do that to each other, they say 'Oh that's old Harry, that's how he always is.' But you know how one's completely different with different people. Which is a wonderful freedom, which is the thing you can only do by seeing people alone.

NELL Do you think men are like this too, or do you think women are particularly different? With different people.

SUNA I think perhaps women are a bit more versatile.

NELL Yes, I think men are more the same. I don't know, but I have a sort of feeling they are. The thing is to be free to respond to all these different things. The difficulty I have is that I become too influenced by the people I happen to get in with or just the environment I'm living in and I think I can be so influenced by someone to think my life is all wrong and theirs is all right.

SUNA Often when one is impressed with somebody, spends a lot of time with them and does things they do, it puts all one's previous ideas into another light.

NELL Have you changed in the last year?

SUNA For the past four years of my life I've been living abroad painting and writing for myself alone, the last summer in Greece I suddenly knew that that floating period in my life had come to an end and that I wanted to come back to London and get a flat, which I've done, and I'm trying to get a job – in journalism.

158

PADDY

*Thirty-one; has a son and has recently
published her first novel*

NELL How close a connection do you feel one's life has
with what one writes about?

PADDY I think very close. But I don't think one should
rush to the typewriter when something's happened. I
think it's probably three or four years later that it comes
out.

NELL You don't make notes, you think back on things?

PADDY Yes. It's out of what one's lived that problems
arise; looking back one realises they're interesting problems and then one searches them out through one's work.

NELL And one creates them?

PADDY Yes. One doesn't report exactly what happened
but one uses the problems one's experienced oneself.

NELL I work an entirely different way. I use notes, but
then I jumble up the notes. Different things that happened
to different people I put happening to the same person but
I work a lot from notes, I write about three times a week,
to quite a large extent about things I've heard or seen before or even read in the newspapers.

PADDY I sometimes take cuttings, cut something out
and put it in. And when I'm actually working on a book
I make notes on the characters. But I don't make notes of

things as they happen to me.

NELL It's very funny because when I am writing from my notebooks I find I can't use notes that happened a long time ago, with notes that happened very recently. Because they don't fit together. It's very odd how what one sees is integrated by the stage one is at in one's own development.

PADDY Yes, your attitude is changing gradually, you can't suddenly go back ten years.

NELL That's right and so what one sees changes. But you're never conscious when you're living, 'I must remember how this felt' in order to write about it.

PADDY No. I think as I get older I do get more self-conscious about that in a way, but it doesn't really happen. When one is younger one is so passionately involved in what's happening, that one just wouldn't do that. One wouldn't think: 'I must remember how this was.' As one is older one is more detached and one is so interested in this whole thing of writing and recreating that one is sometimes just standing aside and watching oneself doing something. Not exactly thinking: 'I must write about this,' but just interested in watching the machinery tick.

NELL This is a great danger I feel of getting older, is that one doesn't care so much about things, one doesn't seem to care even so much about oneself.

PADDY Not quite so much, no. And mentally I find it much more exciting now, one can really consciously develop the lines of one's thought. One can perhaps see things that haven't been done by other people or one is almost certain they haven't and want to go out and try and do them oneself. Whereas when I was very young it never occurred to me that there was anything I could ever do which hasn't been done by somebody else. And now in a small way I find there is my own mental territory which I want to explore.

NELL Yes, but do you find now that you live more in the past and in the future than in the present?

PADDY In the present, yes. In the present and future, not in the past very much.

NELL You don't live in the past? Because to a certain extent I find I live in the past because I'm thinking about the past in order to write about it.

PADDY Yes, I think I'm going to come to this later perhaps. What I'm writing now is concerned with fairly recent experiences in a way, but I'm beginning now occasionally to suddenly plug into memories of childhood and when I was a teenager, things I've never thought about before, and which I'd no idea were in my memory. And I suddenly find them playing through my mind and I feel that probably in ten years' time this might evolve into something which doesn't mean very much to me at the moment. It seems my memory is beginning to grow backwards. It's almost because one has the courage to go back. There's a lot of pain concerned, especially when one was adolescent that one doesn't really want to think about, one is relieved to have grown up and then one can look back with interest after a time. I think now the time is coming when I can look back with interest.

NELL Do you feel any pain at revealing yourself? Or embarrassment of feeling that people will think this is absolutely you, all that sort of thing.

PADDY A little embarrassment I suppose concerning one's family. Certainly not to members of the public or to my friends, chosen friends.

NELL How do you find that having a child fits in with being a writer?

PADDY Well as I've got my mother living with me, in fact it helps me from the discipline point of view because one has to get up in the morning and we have breakfast and then she takes him off to school. And she comes back and works about the house and I have to get on with my work, since she helps me to enable me to do this. If I didn't I would feel so guilty. That's not to say I don't want to work because I do but I'm also one of these people who find it difficult to get down to it sometimes so I have really an ideal situation.

NELL But that's from a practical point of view, what do you think of it from the emotional point of view?

PADDY I honestly don't think it makes much difference.

NELL I sometimes feel that if I didn't have children I would possibly go off and be on my own and be able to sink down deeper into what I thought and felt about things as opposed to giving oneself that three hours, little pockets of three, four or five hours when one is allowed to. That at a certain time one has to come out of that. Whereas if one could stay the night out on one's own somewhere or travel about or go to the country one would get further.

PADDY I sometimes feel this and then I say, 'well, for goodness sake be honest with yourself, you were free and single up to the age of 25 and in fact I never did any of these things which I thought I might do.' I mean I always had a regular job and a regular income and I never threw it up to go round Europe or something like that. Although I'm one of these people who would perhaps have liked to, the fact that I never did it makes me feel I had less freedom than I have now I think. Certainly I think my work has developed a lot since I knew Frank – it's easy to say that I would never have had a book published if I hadn't done because I'm sure I would have done in the end, but I think that knowing him I developed quite a lot and having a child is an extension of being married so I can't really say that I think it's a drawback. I don't think I would be being

162

very honest if I did. In fact, if one has a secure emotional life at least one knows it's there tomorrow – the periods of peace are longer. I never particularly wanted to get married though, and marriage is still something which I'm very open about, to me it's an enormous problem. I do think being single one is every now and then desperate for a companion of some sort, and one does get terribly bothered if one hasn't got one, has no one one can turn to, and at least when you're married you've got your companion, one hopes, and it just kind of relieves one.

NELL Why did you decide to get married?

PADDY Well, Frank was a student at the Royal College and I was assistant registrar there – he'd only been there about a term I think and I really hardly knew him – and I think I helped him to find somewhere to store his paintings and we went out once or twice and one day he just asked me to marry him. I don't quite know why he did it – I don't think he particularly wanted to get married and I don't think I particularly wanted to get married but I think he did it to be honest, to get that out of the way if that was what I was looking for. I just don't know. Anyway I said yes because you know how every now and then something happens very quickly and you have to decide very quickly and it seemed a kind of affirmation of trust I suppose. And so we got married, a few weeks later.

NELL But it's such a haphazard thing whether it works out or not that in a way I don't think it probably makes a lot of difference how long you've known someone, do you?

PADDY I really don't, no. I can quite see some people who've known each other for years getting married and after six months of marriage packing it in. I quite agree, I think it's very haphazard.

NELL Do you believe in marriage in the conventional sense?

PADDY I doubt it. I'm not sure what the conventional sense is.

NELL Well it seems that – in some ways it seems to me very peculiar the idea that one gets married to one man and is faithful to one man all one's life – from the age of 25 or whenever you get married, till you die that you're only going to hold one man in your arms.

PADDY I rather agree with you, and I think that certainly with some people's temperaments it wouldn't do at all. My own experience of it is, I don't mind too much whether men are faithful or not – I think this is another problem. I know everybody says that what's sauce for the goose should be for the gander . . . but I do see it rather as two separate problems. Not so much different from men and women but perhaps different for people of different temperaments. I think that some women they almost have to every now and then express themselves with some other man. They may not have work they're particularly interested in and they've got all sorts of frustrations boiling up inside them which they can only express by giving pleasure to another man. If they're not a hundred per cent fulfilled by their own husband, what else can they do? And I can't see that this is a sin at all. For myself I've been very lucky because I've never met a man since I was married who I wished to go and get very involved with. And I find I'm very interested in the process of a couple developing and getting older and like you were saying earlier, about how a relationship can go on developing. Every now and then it's nice to think perhaps this is something for life, but I don't think I would ever assume much, but I suppose most people do, I suppose that's convention.

NELL I think it's very difficult because of this thing that making love and getting to know someone well and indeed getting involved with people be it a man or a woman is to me the best thing life has to offer. This terrific intimacy, with human beings that one loves. And when one decides to as it were choose one man, and live with them, one can think, well another ten years and men won't want me, and am I missing something? Is one missing something? By not as it were trying to suck the essence of more people?

PADDY Yes. I know what you mean. Very likely one is missing nothing, I think. Our society just hasn't gotten to this stage where intimate relationships can just be accepted without setting up a whole barrier of emotions in people when they heard about it. People can't accept just two people's relationship, they accept it within the social framework, which makes it all so very difficult. And so often people who do just try and have relationships within marriage find themselves got down by the social thing, whether rightly or wrongly so.

NELL Yes. I think this is true because I think that one's emotions against unfaithfulness, although you say you're free from this, is that one is slightly humiliated, to think that some other girl knows about one and is with one's husband, in a way that he's with her in preference to being with you and he knows it, that's the thing that can be irritating.

PADDY Yes, that's terrifying. And I think it arouses very genuine emotions of jealousy and things. But these are completely natural things and how much they're part of this social thing which we've had dinned into us since we were born is very difficult to sort out.

NELL And it works the other way round too. As a girl once said to me: 'I don't mind going round with a married man, but I can't bear the idea that he's going home and getting into bed with his wife.' And that's the one thing that sort of comforts one. If one's husband does go

165

round with another girl, she's probably far more jealous of oneself than you are of her, because one is in so much a stronger position. I feel this, as one has his children, cooks his breakfast.

PADDY And has a much longer relationship yes. I suppose one is always perhaps worried that the big thing of a man's life, one's husband's life, might prove not to be oneself but somebody else, but still I think it's the same for them.

NELL Yes, but do you think there is any way one can protect oneself from being left by a man?

PADDY Most women have this sort of feeling I think of jealousy towards the male sex a grasping – what's the word? – possessiveness. I think that possessiveness is almost a sin and I think that women should work hard in a way to try and get it out of their system. That they should realise that emotional relationships need working on just as much as learning how to cook, and that's a form of protection.

NELL Do you live without any definite moral code?

PADDY I think I do really, yes.

NELL Do you think you know the difference between right and wrong?

PADDY Intellectually I don't, and yet so often intuitively I just do, for me, but I only do for me, and I don't for anybody else.

NELL For you that's good enough?

PADDY Yes. Sometimes one feels so strongly about something one can only say something is good.

NELL Did you imagine say when you were 16 or 17 having some definite kind of life?

PADDY I've been looking back over this period – I can't remember it very well. I don't think I did, no. I think I assumed one fell in love with somebody one's parents approve of and . . . Perhaps by the time I was 17 I didn't, I don't know.

NELL Do you feel your life has got better than when you were that age?

PADDY Oh yes. Well, my parents aren't terribly conventional really by any manner of means but they were living in this upper-middle-class thing, but they weren't in fact very much a part of it, they weren't very social people for a different reason so they didn't have many friends of their own but my father very much wanted me to be a conventional upper-middle-class girl and join the tennis club and go to Conservative dances and things. He didn't help me in any way by introducing me to people who did this sort of thing, but this is what he wanted to do. It's the sort of thing I felt I should be doing because I couldn't see any other way of having any social life and I didn't want to rebel.

NELL No, I agree. But finally one manages to live one's own life. And then one becomes alright. Until then things are terribly hard.

PADDY It's terribly hard finding out what one does want out of life.

NELL Have you chosen your men in the past or have they chosen you?

PADDY Perhaps occasionally I've chosen but then other times it was mutual. I don't think I've very often been chosen when I wasn't expecting to be.

NELL And do you feel you know what you want out of life now?

PADDY On one level yes, I want to develop my writing. I want really to try and search into the social scene in a way, the personal social scene and really try and develop it, the writing. This is on one professional sensible level which leads back to the things that have happened

167

to me in the past, that have been my concern, and that
seems quite human, something I can grasp; but then there
are unknown things that I find so frightening that I – it
just upsets my whole view of the future. I think about the
bomb and race war and that kind of thing, which prevent
me from having a very steady view of the future.

NELL Yes, I find this very much. I find that one's constantly feeling what is one doing shutting oneself up in
rooms writing books when there are plenty of books.
Shouldn't one be out fighting for freedom?

PADDY Yes, I have that feeling a bit. Also I find that
the kind of writing I'm involved with is – a terribly English thing – I mean two authors who mean a lot to me,
which isn't to say that I think they're great writers, they
just mean a lot to me, are E.M. Forster and Angus Wilson,
and there one is concerned in this British thing and there's
people killing themselves out in the Congo – you know.

NELL Yes, when I was younger I used to be the whole
time going to political meetings and completely involved
in politics and then I found I don't quite know what. I
just found that I could be so much more, in personal life
I could wield so much in a way good, in that one could
at least make one's children happy, the man one's living
with happy and that seems to be more than to get involved
in petty wrangles, of politics. Possibly this is because it is
so much easier to have a nice house and look after one's
children.

PADDY I never wanted to be actively involved in politics
but I just feel that perhaps my writing should be more
involved with broader issues, but being restricted to the
English social scene, I just feel perhaps one should take
oneself off and, not necessarily to the Congo, which is just
obvious at the moment, just go to a place like that, not to
report on it or to be involved in it, just live there for six

months and then come back and see what difference it makes.

NELL How much difference do you think money does make to happiness?

PADDY Well, obviously if you're in dire poverty it must make a difference. If you haven't got enough to eat, if you haven't got room for your children, if you haven't got warm clothes for the winter I think it does, but assuming that one has got all those things, I wouldn't have said it made much difference to happiness. As somebody who would like to earn a living by doing something in which it's rather difficult to earn a living, if you see what I mean, I sometimes feel life would be easier with some more money, and perhaps a bit happier, but I don't think it makes much difference.

NELL You see it is very much connected – one tends to connect it with freedom. I find the best thing that it buys for me really is those five hours a day, five days a week which supplies 25 free wild hours. It seems fantastic in fact that it can buy those hours and, at the same time, have a family to come home to, it seems marvellous.

PADDY I suppose yes, it does make people happier because I was just comparing that with my sister who has two small children and her husband is a teacher and there isn't money to spare to buy freedom which she misses very much. But then the alternative is that her husband should gear himself to making money. That wouldn't create the happiness but if an auntie they didn't know died and left them a regular income of five pounds a week just to buy a home help then that would make a difference.

NELL But do you care about clothes and what you look like?

PADDY Not a lot, no. I find fashion very amusing, I rather like it, I'm not the sort of person to dress up very much. If

I had more money I would probably buy more boots and jeans and I suppose it's nice if you're going to a party and you're fed up with your dresses just to go and buy a new dress but I'm not very involved with it.

NELL No, it doesn't seem to matter that much does it? Of course it goes in waves, with me anyway. Two years ago we lived in a completely broken down house and I had a very distinct thing about owning nothing and we had really practically nothing, and a mattress on the floor and – and a few books and cooking stove. And I did suddenly feel that I wanted something better. I don't quite know why I felt this, I felt I wasn't enjoying the child enough because it was so cold and there was no carpet on the floor, I couldn't lie on the floor and play with him, and build bricks and I suddenly saw myself with a carpet and a warm room in a sort of television advertisement world, piling up bricks.

PADDY With nothing on and the snow outside, I know.

NELL That's right. Although I never imagined I wanted a lot of things and of course that's the danger, that when we moved to a nice house, this house, and one began to want to make it nicer. And so one to a certain extent got involved in a material world.

PADDY I'm involved in it from the house point of view actually. I mean we haven't got a house and very little stuff in a way that I would like to have central heating and carpets, I'm not interested in three-piece suites and bedroom suites but on a certain level I would like carpets and central heating . . .

NELL And things like dishwashers that make life really better I think.

PADDY Perhaps, I'm hopeless with mechanical things, I even wash the sheets by hand. I quite like a bit of physical activity sometimes.

NELL And does it bother you if the house gets dirty or the plates aren't washed . . .

PADDY Yes.

NELL But do you mind in other people's houses?

PADDY No. I love other people's houses just because they are other people's houses . . .

NELL Yes, and one is free from responsibility. I find that. It does get me down if I've got a mess. I don't know quite why. There doesn't seem to be much godliness about cleanliness.

PADDY No, I don't know why it is either. In fact I didn't use to have it. It seems to come on with old age. When I lived in a room of my own I think I liked it basically to look quite nice but I never worried about it after that. It got cleaned once a month if I was lucky. But now I notice if the kitchen floor is dirty.

NELL It's the same with my clothes, I hate wearing dirty clothes.

PADDY Yes I do, I don't mind how shabby they are but I hate them dirty.

NELL Do you find communication a problem?

PADDY Yes, I'm not very good at talking. I think I'm a bit better now than I used to be but I find it difficult when there's a group of people having a serious discussion, to say what I really want to say.

NELL I think this is another thing about English people. It's extraordinary how bad they are at communicating, and I think the middle classes this is particularly true of, and how they can die friendless, not knowing the person next door. And this seems to me awfully sad.

PADDY It is. They've been brought up with so many taboos and theories, but they just seem to shut themselves off as someone willing to accept new things and strange things I suppose. You know, they watch the neighbours, new neighbours moving in and there's something rather odd about them and that's all they notice, they only noticed that one little odd thing. They don't notice the pleasant faces perhaps or the bright-looking children or something.

NELL What do you feel about this, as you said in your book, how women only function at full capacity through the medium of a relationship. Do you think it's true?

PADDY I don't think it's altogether – I think it's true of some women. I don't think it's true of all women.

NELL How I would put it more myself is do you think a woman can be happy when she's not involved with a man? Or is that something quite different?

PADDY I think probably very few women can be happy unless they're involved.

NELL How important is sex?

PADDY This is a very difficult question because it's something we've all been made so conscious of – I mean I suppose particularly just at the time when we were growing up, it all came down to women's magazine level, that one must have a good sex life or else one is absolutely hopeless.

NELL I didn't know they had it as baldly as all that.

PADDY Well, not quite like that but I think they do more or less and whereas I can remember as a young teenager it all was something terribly secret and I'd really no idea what it was about and this was presumably how our mothers had it and perhaps never did know what it was about. And then suddenly by the time when we were growing up and old enough to be having a sex life or getting married, it all was much more out in the open, you know, women should have a good sex life. I don't think that it really made such a difference to me personally, I don't think it has but it's kind of given it too much importance. I think it is important but not that important.

NELL I think one of the interesting things about it is that you can't pin it down, it's utterly mysterious how important it is, and that it can seem at some time in one's life all important, I find, and other times really not terribly important. It seems at first with the person you're living with or have fallen in love with it is the whole relationship in a way is involved round the sex but afterwards it's your life together that matters.

PADDY Certainly I think that sometimes it seems that until one's got past the sex thing then relations with the person are going to be impossible. There are some people − people I don't usually like very much − kind of bring it into everything, you know, to interpret one's movements or words or actions as sexual . . . which I can't bear.

NELL Americans often do this. I shouldn't malign Americans but they often have this sort of psychological analytic approach to one's motives, I don't go in for all that. It irritates me very much. Although I think that sex can be a very deep bond between two people when life seems to be getting them down or even when they seem to be getting on each other's nerves. I think it can be something great but then I don't feel it's any more important than sleeping in somebody's arms, if you see what I mean. I remember that at one time I felt that even sleeping in someone's arms sort of love was flowing between you and building up a relationship even while you were asleep. In fact possibly what I think is that a bad sex relationship would matter, do you see what I mean?

PADDY Yes. If one felt that it wasn't true for oneself it just didn't work . . .

NELL But when it's alright then it doesn't matter terribly. I think perhaps this is it.

PADDY It's something which is there but you know, if somebody says that sex is terribly important then one imagines that if they are away from their partner for six months the whole world would go to pot. In fact I don't feel like that.

NELL No, I don't feel that sexually, I feel that one − it matters because one misses the person terribly. And life is so short anyway that if you love someone it's nice to be with them but I certainly don't think that from the sex point of view it is at all important. But do you think that life is primarily a tragic thing?

PADDY Well it seems to have been up till now − yes.

NELL I think one of the difficulties is that one doesn't now know if one should say: 'God it is hell and the only thing I can do is to build some sort of castle around me, consisting of my children and my home and shut myself in this castle where at least I can make things appear to be nice.' I mean that is what most married women try and do. And it's very difficult to know if this isn't just completely wrong and selfish which in many ways one feels it is, or if it's not in some ways a sensible thing to do.

PADDY Yes. I don't think it would be a very good idea to rely on it too much, because then it's very unfair on the children when they grow up. They suddenly realise that their mother's so involved with them there's nothing else for her which does happen sometimes.

NELL Are you frightened of dying?

PADDY I'm frightened of not being ready for it, of it happening before I feel it should happen. I would be terrified if somebody said I was going to die, you know, in half an hour's time.

NELL Yes, but do you think of it physically at all?

PADDY I don't think so, no.

NELL Do you have any religious feelings?

PADDY I don't think so, no. By religious feelings do you mean am I touched at all by any of the religions that exist?

NELL Yes, do you feel possibly that there is a God up there? Is there an afterlife?

PADDY I've never really felt that there was an afterlife and I'm a real agnostic, I just don't know. I mean I feel that this whole complicated universe doesn't sort of spring out of nothing. I feel that we're just a small part of it and there's no particular reason for us to assume that we know it all. In the way we've created our gods and things it seems to me very false. It's this thing of building castles around oneself because reality is so hard, I think. I can completely understand that.

NELL I think human beings . . . I found that one of the things about writing, it keeps me writing, is that I'm terribly moved by human endeavour, I'm very touched by things that human beings do, I'm amazed, and, as you say, I want to explore really why they do things, why they do these amazing things.

PADDY Yes, some people's acts of courage, particularly physical, are terribly moving.

NELL I remember reading about three men climbing Mont Blanc and they all died, one was stuck up there ages and one carried the other . . . one survived, I think it was four, two Italians and two Germans – I cut it out anyway – and one survived and carried the other one all the way down, and he was dead. I don't know, it just seems to me so fantastic and marvellous.

PADDY Yes, I get these feelings sometimes. You know, here we are back in London, one grumbles because one has to wait ten minutes at a cold bus-stop or something but physically we are very weak and nesh, as my mother says, I don't know if it's a real word. One can't face anything, cold rooms or uncomfortable journeys any more. As you say there are these people who can do these acts of physical endurance.

NELL Also a sort of thing of moral courage which I think is fantastic. And that again is the danger of living in your home with your own children and your own surroundings, is that one does get terribly narrow and one is unable to face up to outside things. And one is so frightened of one's world being broken down, so wrongly, I think, overconcerned, about getting a room warm, or getting a cake ready for tea, and that can become . . .

PADDY Yes, because one should always be in a state whereby one could go on living a reasonable life if one say lost a member of one's family. That it shouldn't, in fact, just kill life off completely which in some cases it does. I feel one should be able to get oneself into a state whereby life would still seem valid, without a member of one's family.

NELL One is part of the world, not just of one's family. But do you think that finally one loves one's children more than one could love any man?

PADDY It's a different sort of love isn't it?

NELL It is again a different sort of love. It's a very passionate sort of love, I think.

PADDY It's one that to me seems not open to change – you know, you can't be wavered from it but perhaps loving a man you could, perhaps you could love a man for twenty years and change.

NELL I feel one must be weaned off one's sort of frantic love for one's children at some point because you know, so many grown-ups one knows, I mean grown-up children, hardly ever see their parents.

PADDY I think a lot of parents are disappointed with their children, when they grow up. I mean there's an absolutely stormy period in adolescence where sometimes I think they . . .

NELL Break off relations?

PADDY It does break down their love I think sometimes.

NELL Again particularly I think with middle-class and upper-middle-class people. I think the working class are particularly good at relationships with their children.

PADDY They accept far more from their children. They go along with this sort of cherishing, you know, the girls dressed up as mods and all sort of involved in this pop thing, parents go along with it, not worried by it.

NELL And they go along with a much closer relationship in it, you know I've often heard the children shouting at their mothers, 'you silly old so-and-so' you know, really swearing, and, the mother will whack her across the face and she'll storm out and that'll be that. A couple of hours later she'll be back in again. That just wouldn't happen in the middle class.

PADDY My God, no. It just would not happen. I don't know what it is, it's partly I suppose the way of being brought up. The trouble about it is that the more respect one has perhaps the bigger the gulf. It's very tricky, isn't it, I don't quite know what it is. I think a lot of it's to do with the middle classes until very recently had servants who took the children off their hands quite a lot and the servants were busy training them to a certain code of behaviour and when you're with your child 24 hours of the day you do shout and swear at each other.

NELL I think that intimate relationships are so terrific, are really so much the meaning of life that I want to have them with my children. Is there anything you think you're trying to teach your son about women and how to treat them?

PADDY I'd never thought of it.

NELL I have a sort of feeling about this, because again I often feel that working-class men are better with girls because they've been brought up close to their mothers and know that she's got a headache and make her a cup of tea, you know, that she's got a stomach ache and wants to lie down, you know, 'Oh Mum, your varicose veins are showing' and it's part of the sort of intimate thing which they're good at with women and I would like my son to be like that. I'd like him to treat them well and closely and intimately, I'd like him to understand one feels ill and moody and illogical 99 per cent of the time.

PADDY Yes, I know what you mean — again it comes back to the upper-middle-class theme of either women are put on a pedestal or else they're despised and joked about.

NELL What do you feel matters most to you?

PADDY I like to feel I'm on good terms with the three people I live with, Frank and Dan and my mother. I mean if — Dan's too young to be like that I think, but if for any reason I am a bit on edge about my relationship with either of the others it colours the rest of my day . . . life I think — yes. It's still with me even when I'm out doing something else.

NELL Are you ambitious?

PADDY I think I am quite, yes, I don't mean I want to be a great public figure or anything like that, I would like to do well with writing, I'd like to . . . write good books, yes I'd also like to earn a very good, I don't mean a tremendous, but a fairly good living from them. This would be a great satisfaction to me. I don't mean that I strive after this because it's silly to try and earn money through writing, it doesn't work that way; but I would be happy if through what I was doing a reasonable income evolved. I'd like to be independent and feel I'm responsible for myself materially.

NELL What do you feel about passion? Has it got any meaning for you I mean?

PADDY Yes it has. There's one word — involuntary — that

means a lot to me, that completely involuntary sort of love is very interesting, where nothing else matters, which I suppose is a bit how this relationship was in the book, where nothing in a way can change the feeling of that person as they're experiencing it, as they come within the orbit of the other person, the whole self involuntarily goes out to the other person.

NELL Yes, one finds oneself doing things like walking five miles in the rain to see them for ten minutes.

PADDY That's right. That sort of thing, yes.

NELL But I wonder if men have this thing ever?

PADDY I think they do, yes. Some men don't. I don't think all of them do. Yes, I think some get quite obsessed.

NELL I always feel girls do it more. Girls do more for the man.

PADDY Yes I suppose they probably do. And there's a certain kind of man who does rather attract it. But I do think men do become very obsessed. I think perhaps they aren't willing to act out their obsession quite as much as girls are. Girls really do just sort of cast themselves around and do silly things and men bottle it up and don't act it out.

NELL I think the danger with men, is that they often start off as lovely soft warm passionate human beings as young men, 18, 19, and often through the way our society works they don't have girls then or get involved with girls and have proper love affairs because they've nowhere to go. And often they lose this warmth, and grow colder as they get older.

PADDY I feel this is a possibility. I think it happens to girls too.

NELL Yes, except girls often each time they have a child, they're sort of rewarmed, afire I feel. I felt this very much about having my second child, suddenly so warm and marvellous and having become before that rather calm and logical and practical and you know, interested in a whole lot of things but I suddenly felt full of a new sort of warmth towards life and people. Very much sort of flushed with it, and I remembered very much what it was like having the first child, that it was this sort of sudden – as if one had suddenly been poured full of a new warm liquid.

PADDY It is like that. Particularly if one has a happy relationship with the father of the child and he's entering into it; sometimes people seem to complain so much about pregnancy and seem rather bothered by the whole process.

NELL Having a child on one's own must be very rough.

PADDY And having a child within a very conventional marriage must be rather rough. This isn't very relevant but I've just remembered a girl who had two children – and she just said a remark like, 'Oh well, what poor David had to bear with me during pregnancy' or something, so I said 'Didn't he enjoy it?' And she said 'Good heavens, no, what man would?' I think Frank thought a lot of me when I was pregnant, he really loved me, you know, more than at any time.

NELL Yes, one is gentle, soft, and sitting about and making soup and calm as opposed to rushing around like a whirlwind half the time, and more slowed down. You become very much nicer I think. I never understand why men don't want their women to have babies.

PADDY I think some do get just a bit repulsed by the physical thing because the women do, they get repulsed as they get fat and the men do too.

NELL Yes, but that's so wrong. Really it's so wrong. And this is of course an interesting thing about sex being important. Where I think it's important is I think it's import-

PADDY

ant because it gives one physical confidence and therefore makes one beautiful and this is very true when one is having a baby of the man who one feels loves one's body, is that one feels beautiful. And in a way becomes beautiful. And this is very true if pregnant women look unloved, they look horrible.

PADDY They look awkward. All miserable.

NELL It's marvellous. It's very interesting this thing of women liking or not liking being pregnant. I don't resent it at all, I mean I tend to get a bit bored towards the end.

PADDY Yes, I think I did a little bit. But I enjoyed it – I would more willingly go into pregnancy and indeed having a baby, than having another child there all the time, you know what I mean, the whole process of having a baby is marvellous.

NELL It's the coping with the child afterwards?

PADDY Yes, remembering you've got a human being until death, you know.

NELL Did it worry you before you had a child, suddenly thinking of the emotional responsibility?

PADDY A little bit but not all that much. I felt quite confident having the first one. I think having had one – one obviously doesn't know what it's like until one has had one – would perhaps prevent me from rushing into having a second one. Just the practical problems of coping and help to look after and a bit the responsibility of the life I suppose. If you've got one I don't suppose that two is very much different.

NELL One has to organise for one, one organises the two, I agree I don't think it makes too much difference.

PADDY People often say to me they think it's immoral practically just to have one child, that's something I don't quite understand. I think people are so much independent human beings that they're not going to be bugged by the fact that one has no brothers and sisters, something like that.

ANN

Twenty-nine; has published one novel and is currently in America on a Harkness fellowship

NELL Do you feel you know how you want to live now?

ANN Day-to-day living for me is sort of coping inasmuch as I want to work I find the immediate moment gives one a whole experience, and therefore I hate anything to be very rigid or set.

NELL And would this cut out living with someone?

ANN I've never lived with anyone and the possibility of it is always there. I like being on my own. I find a certain peace and stillness which is necessary for writing and to live with someone would cut in on this always. I realise that to sort of share one's life can bring a whole area of experience. I've often thought what I really need is a wife.

NELL Do you find that living on your own the texture of your life is very rich anyway?

ANN I think it is, yes.

NELL You don't get bogged down in your own kind of routines?

ANN No, I never have a routine. Well, up to recently I've had various jobs and they were routines of course and I found it very very difficult to adapt myself to this routine of having to go into an office and do secretarial work. Habits become useful up to a point but if one allows them and allows objects and allows people to infringe on one's own self then one can become almost static.

NELL Yes this is true but it doesn't ever frighten you, the idea of being alone in your life?

ANN Oh not at all, no.

NELL I think this is very unique. Most people spend their lives trying to get or cling to another being.

ANN Identification mainly. I find one can have a relationship and if one doesn't identify oneself with another person then you have a much fuller experience. I think where men and women go wrong is clinging and identifying so much all the time.

NELL But then what does one do if one gets terribly fond of someone? You know, where does one draw the line if one wants to be with them a lot? How do you say 'well, I don't want to live with you?'

ANN If you get very fond of someone, like Colette did, she said that the greatest thing is always to have good manners with that person and always treat them as if you were not living with them.

NELL But you see I find things like cooking a meal say, for myself, I find this pointless. But it has a point if you do it for someone.

ANN Well, I don't bother at all about meals and if I did live with someone obviously I would, but if I married I would hate to think that they expected me to have a meal there every time they wanted a meal. I would really loathe that and I think women can get very bogged down and they can get bugged up about it.

NELL Do you think marriage is a completely hypocritical state of affairs, nine times out of ten?

ANN Well it seems to be all around us doesn't it?

NELL Why do people go on doing it do you think?

ANN Because of other people mainly. Because of gossip

and talk and it's an easier way out and also for children, isn't it?

NELL Would you have an illegitimate child?

ANN If I wanted a child I would go ahead, if I had enough money and if I felt that I wanted to bring up a child, I would want to give them the best that I could and therefore I feel that if I wanted a child I would have a child. In the circumstances of course at the moment it is pretty impossible.

NELL What do you feel about babies? You don't feel you've got to have them?

ANN No. I feel that it's very difficult for women to cope with a family and to create.

NELL I think this is true, but what appals me is that our society seems to expect you to have children and that in some way you're wrong if you don't have children. I don't know if you've ever noticed this, perhaps you haven't a great deal of friends who've got children, but they almost seem to think of themselves as a clan in the right.

ANN I used to when I was younger. People started speculating immediately and wanted to see you married off, producing children and so on. I think if you make your own terms they accept you. I find this myself, as I'm getting older, people accept me for what I do and for what I am.

NELL Do you think life is primarily a tragic thing?

ANN No.

NELL Do you think it's sad for most people?

ANN No. I think the people, a lot of people, will try and go towards death and everything becomes a drug for them and more or less trying to eliminate some unknown fears, pain and sadness.

NELL Have you changed a lot since you were 16, 17?

ANN Yes I think so.

NELL In what you want out of life?

ANN No, I think I've always known — I think when I was younger, in my teens, I used to try and adapt myself very much to certain societies, the sort of social spheres that I found myself in and suffered terribly, had nausea and vomiting because I felt that I was outside it and yet I didn't know why. I had just not come to any sort of rationalisation at all in exactly what I was in relation to other people. I was very self-conscious of course, and certain people I found I didn't get on at all with and I used to get fouled up about this and worry enormously but as I got older I found this wasn't the case.

NELL But now you feel that you do have a sort of freedom and perhaps this was what I was talking about earlier when I said about control, that you had a sort of freedom to live and to behave how you feel you want to, how it is right for you.

ANN Yes.

NELL This is probably more what I'm trying to say when I say that one has reached that point — one manages to rise above what people think about you because in a way one believes how one behaves is the right way for oneself.

ANN I never regret anything anyway. I never regret.

NELL But you don't feel you've made any big mistakes in your life?

ANN No. Not really. I mean mistakes come about if one has, obviously if one has hurt other people and there again I think it's if one feels one has hurt another person it's really mutual and that other person has allowed themselves to be hurt, and it comes round to that self-destruction thing in them as much as in you too.

NELL But do you have this self-destruction thing?

ANN Yes. I think it's a matter of making much more of that choice, making that freedom that one can either choose to exist or not exist and I think that if one feels that one has lost one's grip on oneself, then one does get depressed and moody but it passes and life then becomes a miracle inasmuch as even to walk down the street and see a child smile and I mean what we all want is some contact to make us feel that we do exist because beyond that there is a complete sort of void.

NELL I think one of the great problems of English people – and I think your book is – to me, to some extent about this – is communication, this lack of being able to communicate.

ANN I think a lot of it comes from inhibitions and verbally we can't really communicate. I find the greatest communication I ever have with certain people is almost a sort of unspoken recognition, where one is not necessarily trying to grope verbally for some contact but you have it there and you recognise it and from then on it's a marvellous mutual expression, that you develop in a relationship and lovemaking can become an expression of this.

NELL Very much. Do you think the promiscuity sometimes comes from a sort of wild thing of trying to communicate?

ANN From loneliness, yes. They always seek complete identification again.

NELL And of course it is a very marvellous thing really to sleep with someone in that one does get very close to another human being. If you like each other that is, you can get marvellously close to someone that way, without a whole lot of palaver.

Do you feel you know the difference between right and wrong?

ANN No. Nothing is ever black or white to me, at all. Evil or good. I mean there's so – almost paradoxical – so much of I think people, when they think how they should feel and this is when one comes up against the thing of whether it's right or wrong.

NELL But do you have any kind of definite moral code? Like for instance you shouldn't sleep with married men?

ANN Not at all, No. I feel that if you feel this complete recognition, then I don't think that any moral code should enter at all.

NELL Do you find you are aware of people's class?

ANN No. Class has never bothered me, only inasmuch that I get sick to death of it being – well, ever since the novel in England has been concerned with class, Osborne and so on, and Wesker. I think it's been overdone. I don't think it really amounts to that.

NELL I think it's interesting in so far as it still to a certain extent activates the way people behave, in many little detailed ways.

ANN Yes. I'm writing about it at the moment, two people who've always had money and have always known a certain side of life and never gone beyond and the girl has never known a family life as such and she's very intrigued by it and therefore, although she hates it, she's also intrigued.

NELL But certainly something that struck me, again when I was about 17 and I began to meet working-class people, was I had no idea how to talk to them, get through to them or they to me.

ANN I hate this sort of thing of setting up working-class people and so on I really do. People are people to me.

NELL They're individuals?

ANN Yes. It's never bothered me that.

NELL But it does bother a lot of people.

ANN Yes I'm sure it does. It exists. There's an awful lot of snobbery. I mean as much as in people, as you would call them working-class, as in people that aren't. The snobbery and all these strata of society.

NELL Are you interested in politics?

ANN No.

NELL Not at all?

ANN In a generalised sense, yes.

NELL In a generalised sense meaning you are interested in justice?

ANN Yes. I'm interested in abolition of hanging and things like that.

NELL And are you ambitious?

ANN Ambitious. I'm ambitious in as far as wanting to go on writing and to know that people will read me.

NELL Do you get a lot out of writing?

ANN A lot. Yes, I think it gives me the greatest satisfaction.

NELL Of anything?

ANN Of anything, yes.

NELL Is your whole life geared around writing rather than being geared around anything else?

ANN I would say it was, yes.

NELL It comes before love?

ANN No. I'd say conflict does come about then.

NELL Do you think we should try to make the world a better place to live in?

ANN I think writers should write and if they go towards what they believe in at certain times, then they should put everything into that. D.H. Lawrence wanted to change the world in a sense, he wanted to create much more freedom – don't you think? Writers do. Russia's very aware of this or else they wouldn't put so much red tape on everything.

NELL How important do you think sex is?

ANN Sex on its own?

NELL Sexual love.

ANN Very important. I think that often marriages break up because there's been a failure through sexual ignorance or just inhibitions mainly, between people.

NELL But you don't think it's just a normal thing that after a certain amount of time people just don't want each other any more, they want someone else? And accept this is just part of life?

ANN I think that there can never be just one relationship. People get married very young and I think this is wrong to get married young because they just don't know what they really want and often people get married because they want to get away from the family and so on and I think they get very disillusioned and the marriage does become very tricky in that respect.

NELL It's very complicated really because I always feel that if two people are married or living together it doesn't really work if they go off and have other people, either.

ANN Sometimes it does, because it might release something in that person and it will suddenly bring an impact to the other person that hasn't had a relationship outside the marriage and they will assert themselves much more and they will – perhaps a marriage will come together, merge much more, but often it doesn't work if the woman realises that her husband is having an affair and she'll go off: 'Right,' you know, 'I'll show you' and she'll go and have an affair herself. Then the marriage will break up.

NELL But I also am sort of horrified by the idea that one should marry and make love to one man and that should be one's whole life.

ANN I agree on that. This is what I'm very much against in marriage that it should be that, that you can't possibly be tied to one person emotionally for the rest of your life. There are so many aspects of love and loving that even though perhaps someone does love their husband or wife they find something else with someone else. And therefore they will find a progression in themselves through this other person and they will become perhaps a more whole person. And yet they will still love each other.

NELL It's just too limiting, isn't it? I feel that one has such a short time to live and then that's the end. If one only has one person, you're cutting off all your fingers and toes, just paring your life down to something so small, that one's life is going to consist of sweeping the floor and cooking and one man. That doesn't seem to me to be right or fulfilling.

ANN I think women, they've been so bogged down until recently – and now they're just realising the possibilities that they have, because they've been so much the slaves of men.

NELL Do you think that women are very different from men?

ANN I think women are very different in many ways. Men are always trying to assert themselves, a certain vanity, and women are not so conscious of trying to assert themselves, they're much more adaptable – they like playing a role that a man will throw upon them, they have many roles, there's a lot of the chameleon in women.

NELL Which do you like being with best?

ANN Both.

NELL You don't find it more fascinating, more stimulating to talk to men?

ANN On the whole I think yes.

NELL Because more of them are sort of freed in their way of thinking and freed out of the kitchen sink as it were?

ANN Yes. But again I find difficulty in being a writer and a woman where lots of men are very unsure of me and they are liable to sort of put me down and treat me from a physical angle which gets me very frustrated and I then try to assert myself and hate myself at the same time for having to do this and I hate the man.

NELL I rather like being treated like this because it's such an easy role to play, the physical role. In a way you get over them by playing that role. Do you find men are slightly frightened of you being clever and think that you're cleverer than them?

ANN Oh yes. It's terrible.

NELL I don't find this, they don't seem to think this of me at all.

ANN Not so much older men, I think they accept one and they're interested and excited and stimulated by an attractive woman who is obviously intelligent. But again I sort of hate the splitting up in as far as saying – people often say: 'She's intelligent too.'

NELL But do you find you change very much as to whom you're with?

ANN Oh yes.

NELL Do you do it consciously, rather enjoying this thing?

ANN Yes. This is the chameleon isn't it?

NELL And men don't?

ANN No.

NELL But that's what I mean when you were saying you don't like it the way men take you as an attractive girl rather than . . .

ANN Well, I would much rather be taken as a person, as I accept them as a person. I used to go to parties and I was writing. I hadn't had anything published and I found that people would sort of nod their heads, 'another girl writer', and as soon as the book came out and I met these same people they were much more receptive and interested in who I really *was*, more than ever before.

NELL Do you feel that's very wrong, a very bad state of affairs that it should be like this?

ANN I think it is. It comes up against a sort of snobbery. I feel very anonymous in the sense that I never get to, purposely, know anyone in the house where I live. I hate the idea. A lot of writer friends seem to have an almost communal existence where they all live together and they go in and have coffee in each other's rooms and they have affairs, and that would completely disturb the stillness that I was talking about. I like to think I can go in my room and shut the door and I'm there and I can go on and do whatever I want without feeling that someone in the house is going to come along and say: 'Let's have some coffee and talk.'

NELL What is it, a sort of big lodging house type of place you live in?

ANN It has eight rooms, each with a sort of gas stove.

NELL It sounds terribly romantic to me . . .

ANN Yes, people have that, you know, I was talking to someone the other day and he was saying 'I envy you your room, your sort of existence, where you can have this room and it's yours and you've got no one to disturb you.'

NELL How much store do you think we should set by past relationships?

ANN I think one relationship might lead to the next – you know, to another relationship – I feel in my own relationships that I progress. That I always seem to gain and this goes back to that I never regret any relationship. There are moments when one does gain and you go towards that in the next relationship.

NELL One must gain by feeling deeply about people, because it must open out something more all the time and make you feel bigger and see what it's all about. What I feel is that anyone who I have loved, that even if I don't see them for a couple of years they mean something to me. They're there. And if they want me or something of me I do feel particularly ready to do it. Because of this. And in other words I do set quite a lot of store by my past relationships.

ANN I always feel it's a pity in a sense that when a relationship breaks up, that maybe you don't see that person. I would really like to still be friends with all the men that I've known.

NELL Do you have any type that you like, or have you been involved with completely different men?

ANN Well, everybody's different.

NELL What I mean is in different worlds or do you find that you tend to get involved with people in the sort of art world, say, for want of a better word?

ANN I have – yes, I think so because of obviously the communication of perhaps doing something towards, creating, painters or sculptors or writers. And a person outside that can often be a relaxation but you can't communicate on all the levels and therefore if one's whole life is geared towards one's work then obviously you go towards people that you're going to find a communication on that level with.

NELL Except that I have a fascination for the strange. The things completely outside my life, and sometimes it would be that that I would go towards. And in an odd sort of way because one doesn't have to show one's hand at all, one is completely hidden, because people don't know at all what you're like.

ANN I don't like that at all. In a relationship I have to be taken on all levels – in fact many relationships I've found have just ended because they have not taken that part of me at all – I've not been able to reveal it.

NELL The part of you that matters to you?

ANN Exactly, yes.

NELL But I think you're a very serious girl, aren't you, really? I can't imagine you having any sort of frivolous relationships really.

ANN No, I haven't had frivolous ones but I would say when I was younger because I didn't, I wasn't aware of, I didn't put much value, let's say, I almost abused myself in this sense. I was physically attracted to certain types of men and I got bored without realising why I was bored. And obviously it was because of the lack of mental stimulus, and if I met somebody who interested me mentally, they physically didn't satisfy me, and therefore I was often up against this dual conflict.

NELL It's a continual duel. It's terribly rare to find a man who is physically appealing and mentally, it's the rarest thing in the world isn't it?

ANN I think if one can find that they, I think respect, this is a word that is often misused, but I think it does so hold a relationship and that if that gets broken off, respect for the other person, then somehow or other nothing will hold it together, if that respect goes or – and often people delude themselves into, they create – I think men are more apt to do this, to create an image round a woman and women too, but women are much more – they hold in respect a man of action, they hold for what they see him do, for what he is doing and they want to be there to contribute towards this. So therefore one comes up against, women like ourselves, the fact that we ourselves are also active as far as creating and therefore we are not so prone to becoming a passive image for the man and contributing towards his part in life. And yet, I am sure, it can become a mutual contribution and one can stimulate the other and make something very good out of this.

NELL But do you find what a man looks like very important to you?

ANN Yes, I suppose so. I mean beauty and the sort of attractiveness is almost a warm thing that comes from within and if one finds one is attracted towards a certain man it's not — I mean when I was younger I was attracted much more by good looks than I ever could be now, in fact I'm very very suspicious of a so-called good-looking man.

NELL Yes, I never liked good-looking men. That I agree with you. On the other hand there are certain sorts of things like beautiful hands that seem to mean a tremendous lot, seem to mean tenderness.

ANN Now gentleness I go for, very much.

NELL I don't know, I think it's a fascinating thing, beauty, I think physical beauty, particularly in a girl, it often seems to mould their lives so much. I think English people are often very suspicious of beautiful girls.

ANN Englishmen.

NELL But do you think this is so, you've come up against this puritanism in Englishmen?

ANN Yes. I would say so, very much.

NELL And where did this whole idea begin, that — I can remember being told as a girl that a man if I slept with him wouldn't like me any more — this idea that they would lose respect?

ANN Yes. Only when I was talking about respect earlier on I didn't mean that.

NELL No I believe very much in the sort of respect you're talking about. But I wonder where the idea came from, it seems such a curious idea?

ANN I was brought up on this. I had a great conflict when I was in my teens, I wouldn't give myself to any man unless I got married. If I'd got married I would've got married at 19.

NELL How did you manage to avoid it?

ANN I think I just realised that it was a whole lot of

bloody sort of social system thing and came to realise that I was a person in my own right and I could choose and it didn't come up to that at all.

NELL Do you think it takes a lot of courage to live how you want to live?

ANN I think so, yes. A lot of determination.

NELL A lot of moral courage in a way, to – not to fall into some pattern someone's set. But do you ever let yourself go, I mean really let yourself go, go completely wild or do you have a gentle kind of life?

ANN Oh yes. I have very much two extremes, where I can equally well go to parties and dance and have a marvellous time – I really do enjoy dancing, I could dance all night and I can drink, I like drinking at parties, and going from place to place and really wild in that way and I can equally well enjoy being on my own but at times I find that doing too much of one or the other has its limits and can become frustrating and then one wants to break out either into going to parties and meeting people and dancing and drinking and so on and then that also has its limits and one wants to break away from that and shut oneself up and come to stillness which it's practically impossible with people, to do that. I stayed out all night in my early twenties. I used to walk around London all night and end up in Covent Garden, and go into the pub there at half past six in the morning. I used to go into a marvellous club near Leicester Square – I don't think it's in existence now – where one could go there Friday night, stay there and jazz musicians would come in from America and just play very spontaneously and you could stay there all day Saturday, Saturday night and Sunday, the whole weekend. But after a while that too in a way got boring if you did it too much, obviously.

NELL Do you get bored easily?

ANN Yes, I think I do.

NELL With people?

ANN Yes.

NELL Not on your own?

NELL Never on my own.

NELL Have you chosen your men or have they chosen you?

ANN I think it's been mutual.

NELL Do you feel that events happen, or do you make them happen to you?

ANN I find that often I'm in, say, a certain scene I find myself in and I have the choice of stopping or going and nine times out of ten I find I go on if I'm really interested. I'm very much up against when there's a moral issue involved, you have that choice before you and you can either opt out or go ahead and I usually go ahead. Because I think of denying, then I would regret, every time. And I feel I don't regret anything I've done because I have always had that choice.

NELL And does passion mean a lot to you?

ANN Passion to me involves communication on all levels, I wouldn't say that passion is just sexual. You can have an intense relationship with a person and this means that you are involved absolutely up to the hilt in every sense of the word.

NELL This is what I mean by passion, sort of heart-to-heart really. What I mean is you're just so – touching. What I find about this is that sometimes I'm overcome with a sort of nostalgia for that passion, and feeling that this is the highest thing we can have in life is this passionate relationship with another human being. And I feel that nothing much else lives up to that.

ANN Well, sometimes I have felt that and then again I've been confronted by perhaps a further intensity which has

been stemmed from maybe finding a certain communication with someone that has sparked off something else
in one and then you go, you go towards someone and you
find further intensity. And therefore there is nostalgia but
at the same time it exists in its own right, the thing of having moments and perhaps this is all that one can have, can
expect. I don't think one should expect too much, ever, or
go back, one should always go forward inasmuch as here
and now, the immediate. You know, what de Kooning
said, 'I'm not interested in space beyond putting my arm
out and seeing my hand or my fingers.'

NELL But why should one not expect too much? I feel
one should expect everything.

ANN No, I don't think so, I think that's almost asking
that – life owes you something. I don't think it does, I
think you owe life something. That you put in as much
as you gain.

NELL Can we protect ourselves from becoming hard, if
we become hard does life become meaningless?

ANN Hard?

NELL Invulnerable, invulnerable to being hurt, and being jealous and being –

ANN I always had this feeling that one should always
retain 10 per cent. I think with a lot of people one would
like to do this but often finds one hasn't and one does
suffer – one gives, gives, gives out and then it's sort of
thrown back at you but at the same time afterwards you
realise that you have not lost really, there's always this
fundamental being in oneself that is retained.

NELL But some people obviously are destroyed by relationships.

ANN They allow themselves to be, they want this, they
like it, it comes round to this thinking what they feel and
not really feeling what they feel.

NELL Do you ever feel jealous?

ANN Oh yes.

NELL And do you think that jealousy is a sort of useless emotion?

ANN I think that with any of these very intense emotions such as jealousy, one at least feels, and it's a feeling and if you feel jealous then you are experiencing intensity of an emotion. If you allow yourself to be bugged up about it then it can be a destructive element in a relationship.

NELL You never feel yourself in a position to tell a man that he was wrong for going off with another girl?

ANN No. I try and understand and I find that I would like to discuss it and try and find out the whys and where-fores and not feel jealous and resent him or resent the emotion but to try and bring it out into the open and to go around it and inside, and really try and sort it out. One is vulnerable only as far as one allows oneself to be.

NELL How can you stop yourself being if you put your whole life into someone?

ANN If you allow yourself to put your whole life into someone then you are expecting everything. Expecting to experience every emotion, if you're up to that sort of in-tensity of feeling that you're giving your whole life to that person.

NELL Here of course I think in a way women are in a very difficult position because if they do either marry or live with someone and have a child or a couple of child-ren, it's almost impossible for them to leave. In that fin-ancially they become bound to a man.

ANN But they can always find work.

NELL Yes. Can they find enough to live on do you think? Can a woman earn enough to live on? If she's got two children?

ANN It is difficult, yes. But it is possible. I would say

that women in that sense have much more to cope with, and are vulnerable.

NELL But you're quite right, it is possible, which is the point. Another thing that I thought about your book was that it was sort of strangely erotic. Do you find things erotic, are you aware of it?

ANN Yes, I think so, inasmuch that the other day for instance there was someone poking their finger in a sort of round ashtray, putting their finger, jabbing it in and out for about half an hour.

NELL I feel that it's a tremendously important thing. It is one of the things that people strike out of their lives. Do you think some people are afraid of eroticism?

ANN I think the fear is something that they never want to face up to, they don't bring it into their own consciousness at all.

NELL And the same really with sensuality?

ANN Is it very different? I think eroticism is more visual – men go much more in a way for visual eroticism and sensuality is much more of touch.

NELL But I feel that both these things are valuable in that after having experienced them, one becomes more open and softer and more alive. And I almost feel that people who don't experience any of these things in a way they're nothing.

ANN They've been involved very much in their environment and the way they've been brought up and they haven't stepped over that edge because it's something they class as vulgar and something not to be touched upon at all, and they're frightened of it and therefore they never allow themselves to go beyond that.

NELL It's interesting how much store people will set by respectability, and how hard it is to break through this. Do you find that?

ANN Oh yes, again and again.

NELL You can't get through this shell and that they are willing to as it were crucify their whole lives in order to cling. But what value do people find in respectability, what meaning has it?

ANN Well, it has a meaning for them obviously. I think that they get caught up in their social environment and they don't want to break out because it's safe. It's safety that they cling to. And anything that's going to shock them out of themselves, out of this sort of set stereotyped way of living, is to be feared and have no meaning for them.

NELL Do you care about possessions?

ANN Yes, except I recognise that so many people become obsessed by possessions and objects that the possessions take over and they become so obsessed that the place and things that they build up in their existence become more meaningful than their own personalities. In that sense I'm very suspicious and I don't care about them in that way.

NELL That is one of the drawbacks of marriage, because part of the married state, again it shouldn't be but always seems to be, is having a place, and leading a life which involves paraphernalia of existence such as cooking utensils. And so it goes on. What seems to me remarkably difficult about life is to be able to live or have one's relationships in a sort of fluid space without picking up a whole lot of paraphernalia as one goes along. It's like having children, having one's children is so marvellous, everything to me, but the whole paraphernalia of one's children, their washing etc, seems sometimes to submerge your relationship.

ANN I find that if you really love someone, or I'm sure it can equally well be with children, that you love those children or you love your husband or your lover and you are concerned in washing, they are part of this person and I think that one can always get a certain amount of satisfaction in dealing with that side of it.

NELL Yes, that's how it should be.

ANN But often it isn't.

NELL I think the whole thing of being a woman, I think this is very much part of it, this kind of sting you know, half the time – I'm terribly mixed up in this thing of babies because I almost feel every fear when I don't have a baby that I've missed the bus. I suppose this is what *The Pumpkin Eater* was all about as you say, that having children is sort of putting a store by, like a store of apples for the winter. But you don't get this feeling, at all?

ANN I don't have that feeling.

NELL But what made you decide not to have a child?

ANN Mainly financial, and in this case I found that I hadn't really loved the man enough to feel that I wanted his child. But, I think that if I did love someone in every sense, on all levels and we had that recognition, then I would go ahead and have that child, even though financially I'd find myself in difficulties.

NELL But did you regret it after having had an abortion?

ANN I didn't regret it because it was something that I'd chosen to do, and there seemed no alternative therefore I went ahead and did it.

NELL But did you find it a very emotional thing?

ANN Yes. Much more so than I would ever have realised. Obviously the whole feminine side of me got the upper hand as it were and the whole physical sense of losing something that was a part of me, emotionally distracted me a lot and created a lot of emotional feeling for quite a time afterwards. What I did find was the whole business of having to see psychiatrists, I think this is something that's so absurd, I mean it is – in fact I was reading that article in the *Statesman* and it's a law for the rich. I think this is in fact something that women come up against so much and something ought to be done about it.

NELL But it's extraordinary how neurotic one is really about the whole thing of contraception as a woman, which I don't think men are, in that there is no safety except taking pills and then one thinks one is going to get cancer.

ANN I think the whole business of contraception is so difficult. It can ruin a relationship.

NELL And to have an illegitimate child in a way that is the end of your life in many ways. It may be a new life, but it's certainly the end of your free life.

ANN Yes, up to a point. I've known some women, painters, that have gone ahead, they've had a child, they've loved the man and he's been married and they've adapted themselves and been able to manage and sometimes they've been very happy, they've brought the child up, and they've existed and found a certain freedom up to those limits.

NELL I think that the factor is to a large extent just how much one loves the man. That is the deciding factor I think.

ANN I think so, every time.

NELL Do you think that abortion can permanently scar?

ANN I think in some cases it might make them very very emotionally disturbed for a long time, I think it depends though on the person, on the temperament.

NELL On how good one is at just cutting things out really?

ANN It can act as a sort of traumatic thing. And yet again it's very easy to (I've discovered with people I've known) – that they have slid back into the same habits and they've found themselves pregnant again and they've had another abortion and so on.

NELL Did you turn against the man whose child it was, rather?

ANN Emotionally I did, but this was very much thinking how I should feel, not really what I felt. This was the complete feminine thing. I went through a stage where I hated him and then one realises of course that it's not his fault, it's a mutual thing. One is confronted suddenly with something that seems very real after almost a sort of dreamlike state one has been sharing with someone and then you're confronted with a huge reality, and you've got to face it one way or the other. And you've got to be practical. I think that a person who is religious would come up against much more, the moral issue in that sense.

NELL Are men frightened of making one pregnant?

ANN No they accept it much more because they're not involved in that way. Although they can get very upset and bugged up about the whole business of trying to help the woman financially and so on.

NELL It completely annihilates the relationship in a way.

ANN Oh yes, it's more or less finished, except of course if they are married, and they have two children or three and they feel they can't go on having other children, they have a life of their own and so on, and therefore they have an abortion, in that sense I don't know how much a relationship stops or goes on.

NELL I do find that sometimes, even talking to you this afternoon, I feel a sort of envy for your freedom, this freedom of having a place and having time and space.

ANN But is it freedom?

NELL I mean freedom to sink down. This I do feel. I can only sink down to a certain depth in myself and then it's 4 o'clock and I've got to fetch Roc from school or cook the supper. Like making dates, I never liked making dates

I can't avoid because I always feel this limits me a little bit more.

ANN But again one can say that in this way, it can create its own freedom because often if one is on the surface to other people a singular girl, singular and single, she seems to have all this 24 hours as it were and not having to cope with things like looking after a husband and children and people say, 'I envy your freedom' but there can be a lot said for day-to-day rhythms that can spark off a rhythm in yourself. The hardest time that I found myself working at writing was when I had a full-time job. I wrote much more than I do now when I have every time in the world.

NELL What do you find yourself doing other than writing?

ANN Seeing people and perhaps I do have that sense of freedom. Say if someone invites me to go and stay in the country, which I love, then I go. I can do that, whereas when I had a job obviously I couldn't and I was very much tied to that and I resented it but at the same time when I did have a full-time job it got me so wound up to that fantastic you know, how one can do, you're working up to the hilt, and you just go on and on but you can't go on and on like that for years and years. Because I had a sort of breakdown afterwards. I was working from nine until six and going back every evening, writing my first novel, very determined to write and finish a novel. I was about 20, 21 and going back every evening and sitting down and conscientiously writing page after page every evening from seven until about midnight and I did this for about 18 months but that was the hardest time I worked.

NELL Are you happier now you haven't got a job?

ANN Yes. Much much more relaxed, much more feeling that I can relax with people because I'm not edgy and feeling I'm wasting my time and ought to be writing.

When one has a job you feel that any spare time one has should be getting down to the work.

NELL When did you ever see people?

ANN Well I didn't. I didn't know anyone when I first came up to London. I was very very lonely but at the same time because I was working it didn't necessarily make me very neurotic and I just used to do the job and then go back to my room in Soho and get down behind the typewriter and off I'd go.

AFTERWORD

What do I make of *Talking to Women* more than fifty years later?

I remember the intense pleasure of these conversations. How we'd sit, perhaps feet up, each end of the sofa, the small tape recorder balanced precariously between us, a glass of wine somewhere nearby, and off we'd go to pin down what we wanted out of our lives and never dreaming for a moment that we may not get it.

This was the 1960s, a time of huge belief in freedom and self-fulfilment. A time indeed for the 'private joys' of life.

N.D.
2018

BIOGRAPHICAL NOTES

PAULINE BOTY was born in 1938. She hoped to attend the painting school at the Royal College of Art but was told that women rarely got in; she went to the School of Stained Glass instead. She carried on painting anyway and also wrote poetry and acted in plays. She married the literary agent Clive Goodwin in June 1963 after a ten-day romance: he was, she said, 'the first man I met who really liked women . . . a terribly rare thing in a man.' What struck Nell about Pauline when they spoke for the book in 1964 was how beautiful she was in a completely unself-conscious way. While she was pregnant doctors discovered a malignant tumour and she refused to have any treatment that would risk harming the foetus. The last work she made, entitled *BUM*, was a brightly coloured painting of a bottom under a proscenium arch: it was used for Kenneth Tynan's revue *Oh! Calcutta!* ('O quel cul t'as!'). Her daughter Katy was born in February 1966. Pauline died five months later.

KATHY COLLIER was born in 1937. She worked in the butter factory in Battersea. She lived in a three-bedroom terrace house nearby with her mother, stepfather, two brothers, her sister and her small son. There was no bathroom and no indoor WC. Kathy was well known for her wit and love of life.

FRANCES CHADWICK was born in 1937. She was the mother of two girls, who were her pride and joy. She also was a furniture maker specialising in old doors that she made into tables. She was married to Lynn Chadwick, the sculptor. Nell remembers getting drunk with Frances once and sliding up and down her enormous bathroom floor.

EDNA O'BRIEN was born in December 1930 in Tuamgraney, County Clare. She rebelled against her schooling by the Sisters of Mercy, trained as a pharmacist, and in 1954 married the writer Ernest Gébler and moved to England. She wrote her first novel, *The Country Girls*, while working as a reader for Hutchinson. The book, which tells the story of two former convent school girls, was banned and burned in Ireland. Edna was Nell's neighbour and Nell remembers them sitting in their Putney gardens in the sunshine and talking about the books they loved. Nell learned a lot from her. Edna gave wonderful parties, and still lives in London.

EMMA CHARLTON was born in 1935. She made costumes for the Royal Opera House and Sadler's Wells Company. Sometimes she would let Nell sew with her and her long bench of co-workers. She had a daughter and a son.

ANTONIA SIMON was born in 1938. She worked as a photographer and loved her Hasselblad dearly. She married a gorgeous man called Ron who repaired barges and they had a son called Jasper. They lived on a barge moored in St Mary's Churchyard, Battersea and Nell spent many happy hours in that pretty churchyard, chatting.

SUNA PORTMAN was born in 1940. After a turbulent love life she married Patric Morrissey, an art historian. They each had three children – Suna three boys and Patric three girls – and together they set up house in Dorset. Suna has always been interested in exploring the spirit and spent time in India on an Ashram. She learned yoga and now teaches yoga to older people. She also follows *A Course in Miracles*.

PADDY KITCHEN was born in 1934. She rejected an offer from Cambridge and moved to London instead, working for an advertising agency and as a hat-check girl at the existentialist nightclub Le Club Contemporain. She became assistant to the architect Hugh Casson and then to Robin Darwin at the RCA, where she met the painter Frank Bowling. Their affair caused a stir: members of staff were not supposed to have relationships with students. Their son Dan was the biggest (at 10lb 13oz) baby on the ward of St Stephen's Hospital, Chelsea. Nell hardly knew Paddy but she struck her as brave and bold and very much her own woman. She wrote many books and made a wonderful garden in the village of Barnwell with her second husband, the thriller writer Dulan Barber. She remained a committed socialist.

ANN QUIN was born in 1936 in Brighton. Her first novel, *Berg*, begins: 'A man called Berg, who changed his name to Greb, came to a seaside town intending to kill his father.' Nell remembers Ann in 1964 as a very excitable person. Her hands would fly all over the place as she talked, about *Berg* and seediness and seaside B&Bs where the sheets were orange fluffy nylon and the landlady brought you a cup of tea and biscuits in bed and the armchairs all had greasy patches on their backs where men had put their greasy heads. She wrote three more novels and died in 1973 after swimming out to sea near Brighton Pier.

First published by MacGibbon & Kee 1965
This edition published by Silver Press 2018
silverpress.org

978 0 99571 621 6

1 3 5 7 9 10 8 6 4 2

Design by Rose Nordin
Typeset in Joanna
Pauline photographed by Michael Ward,
Ann by Oswald Jones and Edna by Aubrey Dewar
All other photographs by Tina Tranter

Printed and bound in Great Britain by TJ International